The Teaching Continuum

The Wheel for Effective and Efficient Learning

Emory

authorHOUSE®

AuthorHouse™
1663 Liberty Drive
Bloomington, IN 47403
www.authorhouse.com
Phone: 1-800-839-8640

First published by AuthorHouse   2/3/2011

ISBN: 978-1-4567-1389-8 (e)
ISBN: 978-1-4567-1390-4 (sc)

Library of Congress Control Number: 2010918479

Printed in the United States of America

ACKNOWLEDGMENTS

Over the years, many people have contributed to this little book; mostly inadvertently as a result of my teaching and working with instructors to help them be more effective and efficient. They put up with a great deal of experimentation and unknowingly motivated me to put this book together.

Specifically, I want to thank my two colleagues, Dr. Randy Swenson and Dr. Ezra Cohen, for their help reading and re-reading specific chapters as I wrote and re-wrote them. Dr. Kathleen Flaherty reviewed my first manuscript and made several suggestions on format and focus that have been incorporated in this book. I owe a great deal to her for her contributions. Mr. Robert Richardson provided many needed corrections as a copy editor and I am indebted to him for his work.

While I have used most of the components of the Teaching Continuum model, I had not used the complete model as described in this book and developed a course in Critical Thinking to test it. Because of this, I owe a great deal to the volunteer students who attended this experimental course. Their help was measurable and resulted in several changes in the structure and focus of the book.

Contents

Final Notes for the Teaching Continuum and the Wheel of Effective and Efficient Teaching

INTRODUCTION

Why and how to read this book

The purpose of this book is to serve as an aid to help beginning higher education instructors learn how to design courses that focus on conceptual learning using components that are aligned to each other as in a continuum. In addition, this book will introduce the Wheel of Effective and Efficient Teaching, which includes how to write student outcome-based objectives, how to design conceptual level teaching experiences with learner-focused enrichment activities, and how to measure conceptual learning. It is a new system that, for the most part, is based on the educational theory of Constructive Alignment developed and promulgated by John Biggs. (2)

Instructors following the premises of this book can expect to be able to develop and deliver their lectures in 15-20 minute segments followed by short activities that enrich the subject being taught and result in a considerable increase in subject matter in the long-term memory banks of their students. I call this the 15-Minute Lecture Model and it will be particularly important to instructors who use, or intend to use, the traditional 50-minute lecture model. In a recent experimental course in critical thinking that I taught, I found that my students quickly adapted to this model, remembered more than they did in my previous 50-minute lectures, were actively learning in every class, and they appeared to like it.

"Whoa" you say! "You're telling me that I only lecture for 15 minutes! Why - I cannot cover all the material that I should in 50 minutes!" My response is: "Yes, 15-20 minutes! And your students will learn more and remember more than in your 50-minute lecture!" Teaching in this model is more effective and more efficient when the focus is on students rather than the subject and when the method follows how the brain works to store and recall memories. Look at the evidence! There are several supportive findings in the literature, and there is a great deal of research evidence demonstrating that students in a 50-minute lecture, regardless how entertaining, lose interest in the lecture after 15–20 minutes of being talked at, even with the ubiquitous PowerPoint supplement. So, effectively, 25-30 minutes of the 50-minute lecture is a waste of time and energy. There is also considerable data that indicates most students leave a 50-minute lecture with up to 90 percent of the subject covered gone from their memory banks when they walk out of the lecture room, and much of that which is carried away from the lecture is lost within a month if not used. In addition, studies on thinking and memory development in the human brain clearly show that being talked at does not appreciably result in the development of long-term memories, which of course, is the purpose of teaching. (31) (22) (23) (26)

"I taught them, but they didn't learn it!" This is a statement that I have heard many times in formal and informal meetings with higher education faculty. This seems to indicate that what a teacher does has no relationship to student learning – that it is entirely the responsibility of the student. This makes about as much sense as having a car salesman say: "I sold him this car but he didn't buy it". (18) A modification of a statement often overheard in faculty discussions is "They must not have covered this in past classes as they sure do not know it now!" This is a common outcome resulting from the 50-minute lecture.

In a nutshell, the purpose of this book is to provide you with a teaching model that does address the problems stated above.

I call this teaching model the "Teaching Continuum," which includes the "Wheel for Effective and Efficient Teaching". There is a PowerPoint presentation as a companion to this book that briefly covers the Teaching Continuum[1] and provides a few examples of concept level teaching; but is mainly focused on how to write learning objectives that focus on the student outcomes relative to the subject studied. The book has five chapters

---

1   If you do not have a computer, or PowerPoint is not loaded into your computer, or if a CD is not attached to this book, please contact me at emory@starwire.net and I will send you a CD or a paper copy or electronic version of the presentation and if paper please include your address.

and each chapter can stand alone or be read on a continuum basis. Each chapter focuses on a different teaching or design concept or concepts that might help you improve your student's attention and recall.

Chapters one and two of the book cover the Teaching Continuum and the Wheel of Effective and Efficient Teaching and provide information about how the human brain functions in its learning and cognitive thinking mode. These chapters provide background evidence supporting the Teaching Continuum design and delivery model. While it provides the reasons for using the model, you do not actually need to know this information in order to learn how to use the model. You might, for example, read chapter three first, which describes how to develop student-centered course objectives; and you might decide to only make that change in your teaching. This alone would be advantageous for you and your students for the reasons explained in chapter one. Personally, I prefer to know how and why something works before I commit myself to change. But, we all have our unique preferences.

As I have mentioned, chapter three relates to understanding how to develop and write learner-based course objectives. In the book, I refer to them as Learning Objectives, but understand that they are performance-based objectives, which include a criterion for student competence and how it is to be measured. The major part of the PowerPoint presentation relates to chapter three, which closely follows and provides expanded information relative to the slides. While working with faculty, I have found the concepts in this chapter to be harder to master by faculty who have had a great deal of experience writing objectives that are subject oriented. Thus having read chapter three first might be a good first step. Make no mistake about it; mastering learning objectives alone will help you use your subject expertise more effectively and efficiently when teaching, but it will require you to change your teaching and evaluation process as discussed in chapter four.

Chapter four provides examples of teaching activities that you might use as memory enhancers for your enrichment breaks following your short lecture or you might use them as your main teaching method and use a very short lecture to give directions, and/or explain the purpose of the activity, and/or relate the activity to previous work or a focus on the future, etc. or in other ways that you might create.

Chapter five covers how to evaluate students for competency, which is what this teaching method requires. This is a whole new world for teachers who have had their entire educational life immersed in norm-based, competitive examinations. This method of teaching focuses on teaching concepts where the students individually learn and individually need to be measured for competence. Norm-based examinations should be used sparingly in this model as all of the literature that I have read, as well as my own experiences, indicate that norm-based evaluations do not validly nor reliably measure student competence.

Chapter six contains a working model that I have developed to help you see how all of this fits together in a course for teaching critical reasoning, for which I am no expert. I will include some data that I found while teaching an experimental course. This was my first attempt at teaching using this new model and I chose critical thinking because I had very little academic background in the subject. In the model, I used all of the conceptual principles covered in the book and I found they worked well as a design and evaluation process and in addition, the principles of learning and retention exceeded my expectations. I also found that I enjoyed the dialogue with the students that this model supports. The enrichment activities were rated quite high as a teaching modality. Of course, additional teaching experiences would refine the model – or any of its parts - and might be an enjoyable educational challenge for beginning as well as experienced teachers.

By way of this introduction, in the narrative, I have described the purposes of this book following the principles of the first step of the Teaching Continuum. To complete the first two steps in the continuum model, I provide the following goals for the book. Slide two of the PowerPoint presentation portrays a model of the Teaching Continuum and its Wheel of Effective and Efficient Teaching.

1. By the end of reading this book, the reader will understand how the components of the Teaching Continuum fit together to provide for more effective and efficient teaching.

2. By the end of reading this book, the reader will understand how a teaching strategy can be modified to better follow the learning and recall functions of the human brain.

3. By the end of reading this book, and with a little practice, the reader will be able to design a course using the principles described by the Teaching Continuum.

Chapter One – The Teaching Continuum

The purposes, course description and goals of this book have been covered in the introduction. The next step of the Teaching Continuum is the first step that directly focuses on the student-teacher phase of teaching. It is also the first step of the Wheel for Effective and Efficient Teaching where course objectives are designed. The objectives for this book are designed as chapter objectives and this designation will also be used for chapters two, three and four.

Chapter One Objective - relating to goal one of the book

- By the end of this book the reader will be able to competently describe the principles of the Teaching Continuum.

Introduction

This chapter provides the evidence supporting the Teaching Continuum model of teaching. In it, I will first discuss the Teaching Continuum and its Wheel for Effective and Efficient Teaching, focusing on how this model works and what that means for teaching. This chapter provides the background and reasons for changing one's teaching style into one that is portrayed in the following chapters of this book. Note: If you want to start by learning how to apply the model, you might jump to chapter three and start working on how to write Learning Objectives and then return to chapter one and/or two later. As I implied in the introduction, each of the chapters in this book can stand alone, but together they demonstrate the continuum.

The Constructionist Theory of Education

The Teaching Continuum is a model that is an expanded version of Constructivism, which is one of several learning theories in education. It is portrayed on slide 2 of the PowerPoint and later on in this chapter. It is an expanded version of John Biggs's and Tang's (3) Constructive Alignment theory that is based on the principles of Constructivism. Constructivism views the learning process as one in which the learner's brain actively constructs or builds upon current and past knowledge. Constructivist learning is a very personal endeavor whereby internalized concepts, rules, and general principles are applied in a practical, real-world context and clearly supports the learning process described in the introduction.

Constructivism is generally attributed to Jean Piaget, who articulated mechanisms by which knowledge was thought to be internalized by learners. He suggested that individuals construct new knowledge from their experiences through the processes of accommodation and assimilation. When individuals assimilate, they incorporate a new experience into an already existing framework. According to constructive theory, accommodation is the process of reframing one's mental representation of the external world to fit new experiences. (6) Accommodation can be understood as the mechanism by which failure leads to learning: When we act on an expectation that the world operates in one way and it violates our expectations, we fail to learn, but by accommodating the new experience and reframing the structure of our memories, we can learn from the experience of failure as well as from other experiences of success. (35) This is important to teachers as it implies using an active method to relate new information to past and/or future information when teaching.

Constructivism argues that the responsibility of learning resides with the learner. Learners construct their own understanding. They do not simply mirror and reflect what they read or hear. Thus, learning is unique to the individual learner. Learners look for meaning as it relates to their long-term memories and will try to find regularity and order in their world even in the absence of full or complete information.

Constructivists argue that teaching is not a matter of transmitting information, but of engaging students in active learning; building their knowledge in terms of what they already understand. Thus, when teaching, it is important for teachers to know what previous knowledge that students bring to the class. Zull points out: "the teacher cannot assume 1) that all students retain identical memories about information presented in class, and 2) that all students retain all of the information given to them in class". (37)

Constructive Alignment Teaching and Learning Theory grew out of an experiment with portfolio assessment, and is based on Constructive Theory principles. According to Biggs and Tang, "Constructive Alignment indicates that all components of teaching are aligned". Alignment provides a continuity that helps the learner better understand why something is important. This suggests that as a teaching session is designed it needs to build on previous lessons, be consistent in the process of its organization, and focus on future learning. For example, "when designing a course the teacher must:

1. Consider what the students already know about the important constructs of the course

2. Develop a purpose for the course that considers potential future learning while building upon known constructs

3. Organize goals and objectives that are aligned with the purpose

4. Develop teaching strategies that are aligned with the goals and objectives

5. Anticipate what students should know about the constructs at the end of the course (outcomes)

6. Develop an assessment process that is aligned with the teaching strategies

This design provides the structure for developing teaching procedures and processes that more closely follows natural learning and how memories are processed in the human brain". (3)

The Teaching Continuum is based on the Constructive Alignment model of Teaching and Learning with the addition of learner focused objectives, which will be covered in chapter three, and a performance standard added to provide the criterion for competence.

In the Teaching Continuum, the teacher must focus on what and how students are to learn, rather than what subject the teacher will teach. The teacher needs to convey the learning outcomes that are intended; by teaching those topics not only in terms of the subject itself but in terms of the learning activity in which the student needs to be engaged in order to achieve intended outcomes. The teacher must specify not only what the students are to learn, but what they are supposed to do with it and to what degree the student must be able to demonstrate the knowledge in order to be seen as competent. In order to do all of this, the teacher needs to write learner based objectives that focus on learning outcomes rather than just providing a topic outline.

All of this indicates that effective and efficient learning is an active process in which students are actively engaged in the process. As some unknown "Wag" has said; "Learning is not a spectator sport!"

The Teaching Continuum Model

The Teaching Continuum model, as shown below and on slide two of the PowerPoint, is a pictorial representation of the Theory of Constructive Alignment. The model portrays the continuity that exists when organizing, delivering and evaluating a course. It is a model that teachers can use for course development, organization, delivery, and evaluation.

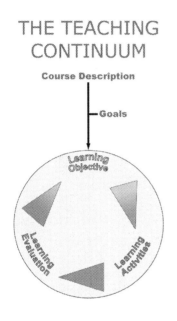

The continuum starts with the course description, followed by the course goals. Since these are two steps that do not directly involve students, they are shown in this model as on a vertical, straight line, which leads directly into three steps that do include students and are shown as a circle because these steps directly follow one another and all together define the teaching experience. The circle portrays the Wheel of Effective and Efficient Teaching. In addition, the circle may be reversed if evaluation indicates the need for change in one or more of the steps are needed. Slides 3 – 7 in the PowerPoint are a sample of how a teaching design for teaching a martial art might look when using the model. (Please note that the number of the slide is located on the bottom of the slide).

The Teaching Continuum Model shows that the first step in course development is to describe the purpose of the course. Traditionally, in higher education, the purpose of a course is established by way of a faculty's submission of a proposal to a curriculum committee that reviews it for continuity with previous and post courses. If approved, the course is listed in a catalogue of some sort and made available to the public. In general, after listing the course purpose, it can only be changed by re-submission to the committee. Hint! Keep your purpose description as short as you can as, in my experience, committees tend to cause the description to grow exponentially.

The second step in the model deals with goals, which must be aligned with the purpose and should clearly spell out what the teacher believes are the major concepts to be learned by students by the end of the course. To create the goals a teacher might ask him/herself: "what are the <u>major</u> concepts that students must know at the end of the course that they do not know at the start of the course?" While there are no standards set for the number of goals, the term "major" indicates that they are big-picture concepts. This limits the number due to time and content. I believe that if one conceptualizes more than four or five goals for a course there is something wrong; either there is too much content to be reasonably covered in a semester, or the goals are more detailed than they should be (actually objectives), or the goals may not be well thought out, or there is something wrong with the purpose. Goals are important as they establish the constructs that drive course delivery. Good goals make the process easier and set the stage for the next three steps, which are collectively referred to in the Wheel of Effective and Efficient Teaching. This is where 'the rubber hits the road', where learning actually occurs, where the quality and effectiveness of teaching is measured and where students are actively engaged.

Step three is the first step within the wheel where student-based learning objectives are created. The development of Learning Objectives will be covered in chapter three and follows the PowerPoint. <u>The PowerPoint is critical for understanding chapter three</u> as it expands a great deal on the continuum principles related to the use of learning objectives. The first rule of writing learning objectives is to make sure that they are aligned with one or more of the goals.

Step four is the second step within the wheel and relates to the development of teaching activities, which must be aligned with the learning objectives. If they cannot be aligned, then they must be discarded or the related objective or goal or purpose needs to be re-visited. This is the point in course development that the brain's natural learning process needs to be considered and, to the extent possible, incorporated into the teaching activities and their evaluation. I have found that developing teaching activities is aided by using the knowledge that all teachers have gained when writing their individual lesson plans. However, when doing so using the Teaching Continuum Model, one has to be certain that the focus is on learner outcomes rather than on the subject to be covered. This can be a major shift for teachers and may require significant changes in their teaching activities as student outcomes are performance based (behavior based) rather than measured by rank position by a multiple-choice test.

The Teaching Continuum, as used in Higher Education, focuses teaching on conceptual learning using higher level thinking skills, such as analysis, synthesis, and evaluation. Higher level learning concepts are not validly measured by norm-based tests. However, some medical schools have adopted a different form of multiple-choice called, among other things, the modified essay model. This is a criterion based question form that uses an introductory problem followed by several multiple choice questions related to the problem. This form of examination is difficult to write but does validly measure concepts, called "mechanisms" in the medical lexicon. Without a doubt, this model can be adapted to other studies as part of the student evaluation process. Models of modified essay question forms can be found in appendix A.

The final developmental step in the Teaching Continuum is the last step in the Wheel and is the student evaluation step. This step is driven by and aligned with the teaching activities. This step is one that may challenge the teacher as learning objectives and aligned activities generally require different approaches to student evaluation than in traditionally developed courses. In addition, learning objectives are more in tune with criterion-based testing than with norm-based tests and as such they are more easily seen as developmental rather than summative, but can be both. Even though norm-based testing is ubiquitous in the current world of student evaluation, most research on measuring competence indicates that norm-based testing does not validly do so.

An important consideration when using the wheel is that the wheel can run backwards. That is, when an activity does not accomplish what it should, or for whatever reason the continuum is not producing the outcomes expected, the teacher may go backwards on the wheel first looking at the evaluation process, then the activities, then the objectives, etc. and fix something or try something else. The wheel will give the teacher significant course evaluation data that will help make the course evaluation more effective as new data is available for making necessary decisions.

The Wheel for Effective and Efficient Teaching

The Wheel provides alignment of objectives, teaching activities, and student evaluation, and doing so enables the student to develop long-term memories that are richer in detail and broader in concept as constructs build on older constructs in the brain. Those enriched long-term memories provide more information for a student to use while thinking and while remembering since enriched long-term memories have many more clues available to make recall easier. Furthermore, enriched long-term memories have much more detail available for the student to use when thinking. This translates into better recall when needed and more in-depth thinking due to the richness of the detail and/or a concept being recalled as the student thinks through a problem. Enriched long-term memories are the cornerstones for competence and impact on the ability of a student to provide quality answers when evaluated.

Wankat states: "Effectiveness means doing the right thing. Effectiveness also involves doing something so that it achieves the right goals or objectives. Effective teaching is, above all, teaching that fosters student learning and ability to recall information. Efficiency is doing something well without wasting steps. Efficiency without effectiveness – such as efficiently teaching a class in which students do not learn – is hollow. Effectiveness without efficiency means the professor, and often the students, waste time. Both are needed". (35) Efficiency is a function of the time on task. The Wheel promotes student efficiency when teachers use the wheel to promote a wider scope of knowledge and longer retention of concepts and details. This enables students to learn more in a shorter period of time and to be better prepared for subsequent courses or practices.

Following the steps of the Wheel promotes higher level thinking skills such as analysis, synthesis, and judgment. Competence testing, a component of the Wheel's evaluation step, lets the students know where they stand in terms of the minimal competence required. This manner saves time for both students and teachers, as each knows what and how much needs to be done in order to reach competence – in short, no more wasting time guessing about what to study.

Teaching activities developed to help students become engaged with their learning are a part of the activities associated with the Wheel. Lectures, enriched by time spent with student interaction, student leadership, peer tutoring, and other efforts designed to help students use the concepts covered in a lecture will enrich the associated long-term memories. The more a neuron is used, the more efficient it becomes and if it is not used, it fades away – usually rather quickly. There are many teaching designs besides the lecture that can be used to help engage students. Chapter three expands on applicable enrichment activities that a teacher might use or modify for use in his/her individual classroom.

Enrichment activities make a difference in learning and recall. Ruhl et al described a comparative group study that looked at the relationship between pauses (breaks) and student learning and retention. In this study the lecturer in the experimental classes paused for two to five minutes while students worked in pairs to discuss and rework their notes and were given three minutes to write down everything they could remember from the lecture. The control group of students was given a traditional 50-minute lecture, using the same room and teaching aids as used in the experimental group. Twelve days after the last lecture students were given a 65 item multiple choice test to measure long-term retention of facts. The differences in the results of the two groups were striking and consistent. Students hearing the lecture in the experimental group did significantly better than the control group. "The magnitude of the difference in mean scores between the two groups was large enough to make a difference of two letter grades depending upon cutoff points!" (32) This difference continued through two years of study.

The enrichment process has been around for a long time. It is how the brain naturally learns and remembers. It is a natural process of learning that everyone inherits. A baby is delivered with hard-wired neuronal circuits that have been designed following the gene orders that she or he inherited from parents. Enrichment is the footwork for brain development which is done as the baby makes decisions relative to its experiences with the world, basically building implicit and explicit memories. This goes on as the child matures and follows a common development pattern in the brain. Basically, one learns what one has to do in order to survive in the world. A metaphor might be construction of a house with the framework representing the gene structure or hard-wired neuronal circuits and the finishing representing short and long-term memory development.

As a Review

1. The Teaching Continuum is an extension of the Constructive Alignment Theory of Teaching and Learning by adding to it concept level teaching with competency outcome measures.

2. The Wheel for Effective and Efficient Teaching provides a cyclical system for course development, management, and evaluation, which when reversed, can be used to evaluate the quality of the course.

3. There are distinct procedures for designing a course. The Teaching Continuum utilizes five related procedures, which are: purpose, goals, objectives, teaching activities, and student evaluation. All procedures are linked together for maximum accountability and student learning.

Chapter Two – Thinking and learning functions of the human brain

One of my reasons for writing this little book is to provide you (the reader) with up-to-date information on the functions of the brain. The story in this chapter covers brain functions that focus on the how the brain handles declarative knowledge. Seeing and hearing are emphasized as these are the main operating senses used in traditional classrooms.

Chapter Two Objective - relating to goal 2 of the book

- By the end of this chapter the reader will be able to describe how brain functions may be used to contribute to more effective and efficient student thinking, learning and remembering.

Introduction

In this chapter you will discover how the human brain works to maintain the processes of learning (working memory/thinking), and how memories are stored (long-term memory). It also provides information that links brain functions with teaching strategies that will help your students be better thinkers, have stronger memories, and improved ability to recall information covered in their classes. The discussion is confined to declarative and functional knowledge as defined by Biggs: "Declarative refers to knowing about things…knowing what the terms of an equation refer to…. Functional knowledge is based on the ideas of performances of various kinds underpinned by understanding. The knowledge is within the experiences of the learner, who can put declarative knowledge to work by thinking and solving problems." (2) Seeing and hearing are emphasized in this chapter because these processes are the main brain functions involved in learning found in traditional classrooms; acknowledging that learning and recall are involved with other brain functions to a lesser degree.

The Human Brain

The human brain is the center of the human nervous system and is considered to be the most complex mechanism in the known universe. (22) The adult human brain weighs on average about 3 pounds. There are several distinct parts to the brain. For the purpose of this discussion, the discussion will focus mainly on the cerebrum, mid-brain, optic lobe, and the cerebellum.

According to Gross a primitive human brain evolved over millions of years, building on brains that had evolved over the millions of years prior to man. Continued evolution of the primitive brain resulted in added new lobes and functions into a design similar to the one that developed in lizards and crocodiles. In the literature it is called the "reptilian brain." This oldest part still remains as part of the human brain, albeit, considerably modified. It includes the brain stem, basal ganglia, reticular activating system, and the midbrain to make up the stem of the human brain. (15)

The mid-brain evolved from the reptilian brain after an additional millions of years, as mammals became the dominant species on earth. The mid-brain literally wraps around the reptilian brain area. In humans the mid-brain is where implicit memories are stored as long-term memories. These include implicit belief memories that we use when making decisions and/or evaluating and are important relative to their use when reasoning. (30)

The mid-brain plays a role in the sense of seeing and hearing, something that makes this area important to didactic learning. The mid-brain monitors all our sensory input, converts it into appropriate modes for processing, and directs it to an appropriate memory-storage system. Neurochemicals in the mid-brain also affect our ability to transfer memories from working memories to long-term memories. Unless that transfer takes place we literally lose what we are thinking about within 7 (5-12) seconds, which is the time it remains in working memories. (31) (22) (23) (26) It appears that the working memories that survive are those related in some way to one's long-term memories. Memories fade away if not used and reinforced.

The Thinking Brain

A third section of the brain is the distinctively human cerebrum and is the latest neurological evolutionary development in the brain that some say is still evolving. It is the largest part of the human brain and is significantly larger than those of other primates. It lies at the top of the brain stem with both sides and back surrounding the mid-brain. This part of the brain is where much of our mental activity happens. Spatial, declarative, emotional thinking and dreaming, judging, remembering, processing, and decoding sensory information all pass through this area.

When new information arrives at the brain it is processed by the brain by adding the new data to the information already in long term memories residing in the brain. Long-term memories involved in the new learning are changed and strengthened by new, congruent memories making them easier to retain and to be accessed by new, related learning. Neurons in the brain that are not used are discarded or fade away (33) and this is another reason for teachers to use enrichment activities. This process is pretty straight forward and has been validated by several different research studies made since the 1970s. This use it or lose it process continues throughout life and is a mechanism that is of great importance to educators as it implies several things related to the process of teaching. It is well established that new and added experiences have a major role in establishing memories and memory enhancement. (31)

Researchers believe that long term memory retrieval, like long term memory, may involve constructive processes, which is demonstrated by how the brain lights up during recall using specific imaging techniques. That is, a long term memory uses parts from many other memories as recall takes place. What this implies is that long-term memories become stronger with use as enrichment activities add more information to them. This relates to the need for enrichment activities while teaching. Individuals retrieve only a portion of the information that has previously been presented to them; on some occasions, they may fill in the holes of their memory based on what is logical or consistent with their existing frames and knowledge about the world. This mechanism of the brain supports the idea of the uniqueness of individual memories. (23)

Recent brain research outcomes strongly support the principles of Constructivism introduced by Piaget in the 1930s. Advanced imaging techniques portray a very active brain when one is thinking, learning, and recalling. Major centers in the brain are involved with these thinking and learning functions. Various portions of the brain show considerable activity while other portions, all over the cerebellum, are simultaneously active. These processes are thought to represent the constructive activity of accommodation involved with learning, but more research still needs to be done in order to clearly explain how it works. This appears to be somewhat of a contradiction of the long held hypothesis that long-term memories are held in a single structure resembling a hologram. For more information on holograms see appendix B.

When we hear a sentence, we develop an image of what it describes. If we later remember the image we may remember what the sentence was about, but not the exact words. In like manner, if we view a picture of

Yosemite Falls we may describe to ourselves what our brain has marked as significant details of the picture but other details will be lost. Research and common sense indicates that the more the memory is used the more detail that can be described and the easier it is to access the memory. Remembering detail for declarative memories can happen only if the detail has been saved as an important part of a frame called a schema. This brain activity has important implications for the design and delivery of teaching activities and student evaluation activities.

The most common description of long-term memory hypothesizes that a long-term memory looks something like a three dimensional picture (hologram) of one's experience. The picture may contain the schemas related to declarative knowledge along with associated schemas that arise from the other senses, such as emotion, tactical, touch, odors, as well as perceived importance, and neuronal strength. This indicates that the long-term memory does not exist as a "bit" in computer jargon, but has a more amorphous existence. However, there is hierarchy in the schemas of long-term memories, which relate to the importance of individual frames and this hierarchy seems to be generated by the number of times that a particular frame is used in the learning experience. This explains why people remember different things about a similar experience. Teachers should remember this when teaching and evaluating students. Repetition of a concept by use of different methods of teaching helps students consolidate long-term memories by strengthening the nerve bundles associated with the memories. (30)

The Eyes and Ears

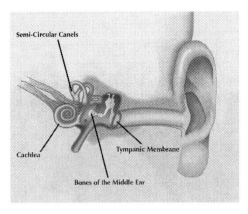

The visual and hearing senses are emphasized in this book because they are the senses that are basic relative to the traditional approach to teaching the 50-minute lecture. The teacher talks and often supplements the talk with paper handouts, pictures, drawings, PowerPoint presentations, computer simulations, etc. The student sees and hears and, in general, hearing is the sense predominantly used, but all other senses such as feelings, touch, hunger, etc. are active at the same time, and all of this may become part of long-term memories and are often used in recall.

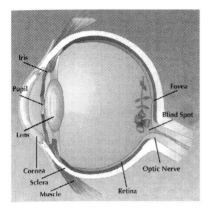

The act of seeing starts when the lens of the eye focuses an image from the environment onto a light-sensitive membrane in the back of the eye called the retina. The retina is actually part of the brain that is isolated to serve as a transducer for the conversion of patterns of light into neuronal signals. The lens of the eye focuses light on the photoreceptive cells of the retina, which detect the photons and wave lengths of light and respond by producing neural impulses. These signals are processed in a hierarchical fashion by different parts of the brain, from the retina to the thalamus, and to the primary and secondary visual cortex located in the cerebrum. How signals are actually processed remains a puzzle and significant research is on-going at the present time. However, the storage of visual memories is known to reside primarily in the occipital lobe of the brain and perhaps briefly in the thalamus and/or the hippocampus (30), which are parts of the mid-brain.

The human sound gathering system is composed of three main parts made up of the outer ear, the middle ear, and the inner ear. For the most part, sound follows a pathway from the outer ear through the middle and inner ear and may end up as part of the brain's memory system. From the outer ear sound, in the form of pulses and waves, enter the auditory canal, which amplifies sounds that are between 3 & 12 kHz. At the far end of the canal is the eardrum (or tympanic membrane) that marks the beginning of the middle ear. In the middle ear the sound waves travel through a series of bones that convert the lower pressure eardrum sound vibrations (waves) into higher pressure, pulsing waves to another, smaller membrane called the oval window that is the window to the inner ear.

The inner ear consists of the cochlea and several non-auditory structures. The traveling sound is converted from the pulse in a wave form to nerve impulses in the cochlea. The Organ of Corti of the cochlea, a small snail-like structure, forms a ribbon of sensory epithelium which runs lengthwise down the entire cochlea and includes hair cells as a mechanism to transform the pulses into nerve impulses. From the cochlea the nerve impulse travels down nerves and eventually reaches the thalamus, and from there it is relayed to the auditory cortex. In the human brain, the primary auditory cortex is located in the temporal lobe. The primary auditory cortex is the first region of the cerebral cortex to receive auditory input. The cortical region is responsible for interpreting the sensation of basic characteristics of sound such as pitch and rhythm and for the processing of acoustical signals so that they can distinguish speech, music, or noise. (30)

The signals from the auditory cortex of the temporal lobe are sent to the thalamus where it is judged meaningful or not. If meaningful, it is sent to the frontal lobe where it is judged again by way of the working memory system. The parts of the signal that survives is made, along with input from other senses, into a long-term memory and stored in various places in the cerebellum and perhaps, the mid-brain, limbic system. How such memories are actually stored remains a mystery and continues to be an open question.

While the sense conduction process for both the eye and the ear are very well known, the working and storage mechanisms are not. We know where in the brain these activities take place during long-term memory integration, but we do not yet know exactly how the memories are stored other than they are stored as a long-term memory (holistically). However, there are solid theories of learning that explain the integration of new memories with the old memories stored as long-term memories. (Mostly because of rats and mice)! But, we only make guesses as to what a long-term memory really is. Never-the-less, the use of the constructive theory of learning when teaching supports what we know about learning and memories. (8) (2) We can say that it is important for teachers to recognize and utilize the concepts of the constructive theory, or one of its derivatives such as the Teaching Continuum, as a guide to enrich their teaching effectiveness and efficiency.

When new sensory information arrives in working memory it may be primarily from the ear, but other senses are always involved. All senses about an experience arrive in working memory at the same time from different parts of the body using different routes. If a premise becomes a part of a long term memory it is stored in a schema in what appears to be a hierarchy sorting out the different senses, perhaps by importance, but no one actually knows the scaffolding process. The sense that is judged in some way to be most important is higher on the hierarchy scaffolding and takes priority over the weaker senses. In teaching, the emphasis given to declarative information probably is the reason it is judged as highest on the hierarchal scaffold. Other senses, such as an emotion that accompanies the sensory information, senses sent from the skin relative to the environment in which the original sense occurred, accompanied distractive noise, mood of the person involved, etc. etc. All of the additional information that accompanies the main sensory stream makes up the long-term memory established in an importance, hierarchical manner. (30)

Recall of a memory arrives at the working memory (while thinking) somewhat like a picture with the main sense in the foreground and the minor senses in the background; i.e. a concept picture made up of details. Because of this structure teachers must be aware that recall is unique to the person and the same memory in others can be recalled quite differently depending upon its unique position on the individual brain importance scaffolding.

Of importance to the teacher is a process called memory enhancement. Enhancement occurs every time the memory is used and the more it is used the more the memory is enhanced, which means that it is made stronger. The strength of a long-term memory (an enhanced long term memory) is directly related to 1) ability to recall and 2) the length of time that the memory remains active in the brain. The more it is used, particularly if the teaching technique used varies somewhat and is repeated, the stronger the memory becomes. If it is not used, it fades away. (20)

The concept of enrichment discussed in this book is not a new concept in education. Elementary teachers often use enrichment activities when teaching; generally giving directions and then asking students to do or create something. Technical teachers, physical education teachers, Science teachers, and others often used the model, although they may call it something else. However, other than the ones discussed above, high school and higher education teachers rarely use enrichment activities in which students work with each other to learn and retain concepts, which is what this book's model does.

Teachers should find ways to provide teaching activities that support strengthening the long-term memories. In doing this, they become more effective (students have better recall) and efficient (the memory lasts much longer so it does not need to be re-taught). In addition, this type of active learning helps students take more responsibility for their learning as responsibility can be built into the lesson plan through teaching activities.

Zull alludes to this responsibility when he says: "Our experience comes from outside the brain, but the brain has the ability to turn that outside experience into knowledge and understanding. The new knowledge comes from within. We no longer need to repeat, or even remember, exactly what we experienced from the outside. I suggest that this is the essence of what we mean when we speak of taking ownership of knowledge. It is a *change in the learner* from a receiver to a producer. Since we do not have to wait for new information to arrive on the outside for understanding, we do not have to wait for new information to arrive to deepen our comprehension. We can move from passive to active and become creators of knowledge". (37)

As a Review

1. The human brain seems to construct knowledge by adding new knowledge from short-term memory while linking to old knowledge found in long-term memories.

2. Long-term memories are stored in distinct portions of the human brain depending upon the nature of the stimulus that triggered the short-term memory.

3. All memories fade away and/or are lost if they are not used and the more they are used the stronger the memory becomes.

4. Long-term memories will be retained longer by varying the teaching activities to include enrichment activities.

5. Most of the short-term memories are lost within 5-20 seconds if not associated with a long-term memory.

6. Long-term memories will be recalled more effectively and efficiently when the enrichment activities included original concepts studied and personally developed by students.

Chapter Three – Introducing learning objectives

Chapter three objectives – relating to goal 2 of the book

1. By the end of this chapter, the reader will be able to compose a brief explanation of the evolution of learning objectives in education with quality of the explanation defined by the instructor.

2. By the end of this chapter, the reader will be able to competently describe the rationale supporting the use of learning objectives rather than traditional, content-based objectives.

3. By the end of this chapter the reader, when given traditional, content focused objectives, will be able to competently transform the objective statement from content orientation to student orientation by use of the learning objective model.

Introduction

In this chapter, we will focus on step three which is the first component of the Wheel for Effective and Efficient Teaching. This chapter alone will be a major help for you to become a more effective teacher. It will focus on developing Learning Objectives for a course. The discussion will closely follow slides 13-22 in the PowerPoint presentation that supports this chapter. Other slides in the presentation will show how learning objectives fit into the Teaching Continuum model. (Note: As indicated in the introduction, the PowerPoint is critical to understanding this chapter. If a CD is not found on the back cover of this book, please email emory@starwire.net and request an CD or an electronic copy or a paper copy).

First, a little background on the evolution of objectives

The precursor of objectives in teaching occurred in the little one room school house that was ubiquitous to the countryside in the 1800s. Teachers in the early one-room schools were extremely busy with responsibility for four or more subject areas and with up to eight grade levels. Teachers at that time either had to quickly learn how to manage or they would be replaced for not controlling the students in the school. Partially because of this, planning via lesson plans became a standard. This activity can be thought of as the genesis of educational objectives.

Over the years, along with industrialization and the evolving of factory-like schools in the bigger cities, objectives began to take the look of management schedules, where content was emphasized as the main focus of learning. This type of objective focus continues to be used today in many current institutions of higher learning and other schools.

In the early 1900s, social psychologists became interested in learning and their learning theories became a part of education evaluation strategies. New styles of objectives were developed in order to accommodate the developing theories and during the mid 20th Century, objectives began to segue from a focus on content to a focus on the learner outcomes as the product of education, particularly in the technical schools. (18) Performance-based objectives were an outcome of this growth and are used sometimes in liberal arts and professional, education institutions today; but more often content type objectives are used. However, this movement did introduce the concept of competence into education and the necessity to teach content concepts rather than the details of content alone and this was a good step.

There is considerable evidence in educational and psychological research that competence is strongly related to long-term memories and recall. This is thought to be due to differences between detail learning and concept learning, because the details that are found in working memories do not become a part of long-term memories unless they are part of a larger concept. This is the reason why the use of learning objectives are important in education by changing the focus of learning from learning factual content to learning how factual information can be used to form concepts.

What are Learning Objectives?

Learning objectives are an evolution of the performance (sometimes called behavioral) type of objective, which contains all of the principles of the performance objective, but adds a criterion of competence as a part of the objective. Learning objectives are not content objectives, because they focus on student outcomes and not content only. Of course, they have a content component, but they focus on the student first and content follows. A criterion in a learning objective is a standard of competence that the student needs to reach in order to be seen as competent. Adding the criterion is seen as a motivating device for students as they may track their personal progress during the course. Student motivation is one way, of many, to provide for more effective and efficient learning as student motivation and in the research literature it has been shown to be a positive factor in higher student outcomes.

So - How do we go about writing learning objectives?

I recommend that you use slides 13 through 22 of the PowerPoint presentation to help you understand what learning objectives are all about and how to write them. Slides 5 and 26 also give examples of learning objectives as part of the Wheel of Effective Teaching and Learning.

Slide 13 identifies three general strengths of the learning objective; 1) learning objectives establish a focus on the student rather than the course, 2) guides the instructor relative to the planning of instruction and evaluation of student achievement, 3) guides the learner on what to study, how to study, how to prepare for tests, and what one needs to be able to do to be deemed competent. The three are not all inclusive. Other strengths include:

- They show colleagues and students what we value

- They guide the learner relative to self-assessment

- They provide the basis for analyzing the cognitive thinking we are expecting from the learner

- They make teaching more focused and organized

- They provide a model so that students can write their own objectives and this helps develop an important life-long learning skill; the setting of personal objectives (17)

Slide 14 provides a description of the four parts of a learning objective. They are: 1) a description of the content (task(s) to be studied), 2) a description of the conditions required for demonstrating learning, 3) a description of the performance required in order to evaluate competence, and 4) a description of the criteria (standard) to be achieved in order to be considered competent. In order to be called a learning objective all of these parts must be found in the objective statement. The following is an expansion of the four parts.

1. **Description of task to be studied**: The objective covers any content knowledge that is pertinent to the goal under which the objective is developed. This is very similar to the traditional content objective.

2. **Conditions required for learning**: An objective should describe the conditions under which the learner will be

expected to perform in the evaluation situation; i.e. what tools, references, other aids, time, etc., will be available. What will be provided or denied or constrained must be clear.

3. **Performance required**: The key to the performance is the use of an active verb to describe the performance; i.e. **define, describe, identify, interpret, evaluate, etc**. There are hundreds of active verbs.

4. **Criterion for competence**: This is a standard of performance that indicates whether or not the performance meets the requirement for competency. (14) This is a pass/fail situation, which might be expanded using a scaled continuum such as novice competent, expert, superior, etc., depending on growth beyond competence, with appropriate standards established for each level. This concept is discussed in chapter five.

Learning objectives are concept based and the associated teaching activities reflect this change. This suggests that learning objectives support the way the brain works, making the student learning more effective and efficient. It also indicates that the verb used in learning objectives is an **active verb,** which is one that refers to an action of some sort by the learner. (17)

The definitions of the active verbs listed in 3 above are:

To **DEFINE**: To stipulate the requirements for inclusion of an object, word, or situation in a category or class. Elements of one or both of the following must be included: (1) the characteristics of the words, objects, or situations that are included in the class or category; (2) the characteristics of the words, objects, or situations that are excluded in the class or category. To define is to set up criteria for classification.

To **DESCRIBE**: To name all of the necessary categories of objects, object properties or even properties that are relevant to the description of a designated situation. The objective is in the form "the student will describe this order, object, or event" and does not limit the categories that may be used in mentioning them. Specific or categorical limitations, if any, are to be given in the performance standards of each objective. When using this as a verb, it is helpful to include a statement to the effect of what the description, as a minimum, must reference.

To **IDENTIFY**: To indicate the selection of an object of a class in response to the class name, by point, picking up, underlining, marking, or other responses.

To **INTERPRET**: To translate information from observation, charts, graphs, and written materials in a verifiable manner.

To **EVALUATE**: To classify objects, situations, people, conditions, etc., according to defined criteria of quantity. Indication of quality must be given in the defined criteria of quality of each class/category. Evaluation differs from general classification only in this respect.

To obtain lists of active verbs, I recommend that you go on line and query "active verbs" and/or see appendix C.

Slides 15 through slide 22 provide samples of traditional content objectives and learning objectives. Slide 15 shows samples of typical traditional objectives and slide 16 shows samples of learning objectives. The four parts of learning objectives are shown in color with blue-green representing the conditions, underlined blue-green representing the required performance, and red representing the competence and criterion standard required to demonstrate competence. Note that in learning objectives the competency and the standard are often together.

An explanation for slide 16 using the second objective on the list; "given a stethoscope and a clinical environment" states the conditions, "the students will be able to ...... diagnose a heart arrhythmia" states the performance required, "correctly" is the competence level, and "in 90 % of affected patients" is the criterion standard.

Slides 17 and 18 positions the traditional content objectives first and then provides a re-write of the objective in learning objective form following the first. Note that the different parts are colored as we found in slide 16. You will also note that learning objectives are generally more "wordy" than those that are content-based only. The components are similar in style to slide 16. Note also that the learning objective converts the factually focused content objective to a concept focused objective, which explains in part the added number of words.

A Little More Practice

On the next few pages there are ten examples of learning objectives written for different types of subjects and providing different styles of learning objectives. As you review these, consider that the wording in each example might change as to task, condition, and performance, and the criterion would be established for each. Note that the task and the performance are similar in these examples. For each of the following, the learner objective is written out followed by samples of the four parts of the objective; the task (content covered), the condition, the performance, and the criterion for competence. Consider that each of the questions may be asked in different ways and still be a valid concept statement.

1. When given a drawing of two brain neurons the student must be able to accurately describe the energy exchange process that occurs when a bit of information moves from one neuron to another.

Task: Describe the energy exchange process that occurs when a bit of information moves from one neuron to another

Condition: when given a drawing of two brain neurons

Performance: the student must describe

Criterion: accurately.

2. Given a golf ball, the student must be able to accurately write the vector equation that results from applying Newton's Second Law to the golf ball.

Task: Write a vector equation

Condition: given a golf ball

Performance: applying Newton's Second Law to a golf ball

Criterion: accurately.

3. Given several of the environmental problems discussed in class, the student must be able to competently describe relationships between human health and four of the environmental problems.

Task: Describe relationship between human health and environmental problems

Condition: given several of the environmental problems discussed in class

Performance: describe relationships

Criterion: competently.

4. Given a concept problem in logic, the student must be able to correctly describe the synthesis reasoning required to solve the problem.

Task: Describe synthesis reasoning

Condition: given a concept problem in logic, the student must be able to

Performance: describe synthesis reasoning required to solve a problem

Criterion: correctly.

5. Upon completion of this unit, the student must be able to correctly describe the mechanisms of action, the pharmacological effects, and the adverse effects of lithium on human systems.

Task: Describing mechanisms of action, pharmacological effects, and adverse effects of lithium on human systems

Condition: upon completion of this unit

Performance: describe the mechanisms of action, pharmacological effects, and adverse effects of lithium on human systems

Criterion: correctly.

(Note: This question is probably too detailed for a good learning objective as there probably are a number of elements with similar mechanism effects. As is, it would require many objectives of similar design to measure the mechanism issue. And as is, it is not focused on concepts. *The concept might be mechanism affects*).

6. By the end of the course, and provided with the necessary equipment, the student must be able to intubate a patient with

minimum discomfort to the patient; competence to be judged by the attending physician.

Task: Intubate a patient

Condition: by the end of the course, and provided the necessary equipment,

Performance: the student must be able to intubate a patient with minimal discomfort.

Criterion: competence judged by the attending physician.

7. At the end of the basic science portion of the medical curriculum, the student will achieve a criterion score of above 95 percent correct on 100 multiple choice questions relating basic science knowledge of the mechanisms of human health.

Task: basic science knowledge of the mechanisms of human health

Condition: at the end of the basic science portion of the medical curriculum

Performance: achieve a criterion score on a 100 question multiple choice test

Criterion: a score above 95% correct.

8. By the end of the 3rd year and given appropriate equipment, the medical student must be able to competently describe the routine technical procedures of venipuncture, inserting an intravenous catheter, arterial puncture, thoracentesis, lumbar puncture, inserting a Foley catheter, and suturing lacerations with competence criteria set by a panel of experts.

Task: Describe routine technical procedures

Condition: by the end of the 3rd year and given appropriate equipment

Performance: the medical student must be able to competently describe the routine technical procedures of venipuncture, inserting an intravenous catheter, arterial puncture, thoracentesis, lumbar puncture, inserting a Foley catheter, and suturing lacerations.

Criteria: competence criterion set by a panel of experts.

9. Given a print-out for the analysis of a multiple-choice exam the student will be able to correctly describe the validity and reliability of the test scores for each question.

Task: Describe validity and reliability of test scores for each question

Condition: given an item-analysis print-out of a multiple-choice exam

Performance: describe the validity and reliability of the test scores for each question

Criterion: correctly.

10. Prior to graduation, an intern must be able to competently describe the principles that govern ethical decision making that arise at the end of life.

Task: The student must be able to describe the principles of ethical decision-making that arise at end of life

Condition: prior to graduation

Performance: describe the principles that govern ethical decision making that arise at end of life

Criterion: competently.

Whew! But before you leave this discussion, go back to slides 3-6 and 24-26 to review how the learning objective fits into the Wheel of Effective and Efficient Teaching and how this drives the teaching activities process that will be covered in the next chapter and then find some content objectives and 1) re-write them as concepts and 2) convert them into learning objectives. If you run into trouble and would like some help, look at the final slide in the PowerPoint presentation.

For Your Enjoyment or Other Emotions:

I have added a few typical, traditional course objectives that you might wish to play with to convert them to Learning Objectives as I have defined them.

1. Each learning objective needs to have the four components of learning objectives.

2. You will need to consider what the learner focus should be for each objective – which means that you will have to re-write the objective using your own ideas.

3. Some statements are too broad for being called an objective and will need to be to be broken into one of its parts in order to write an objective (as stated, it is probably a goal).

4. There are many ways that they can be re-written and still be valid depending upon the expected outcome(s).

5. If you need help or just want to show how smart you are, please contact me at emory@starwire.net and we will exchange e-mails.

A list of traditional objectives

In this course:

1. We will study the photosynthesis cycle in the leaves of green plants.

2. We will cover the Animal Kingdom.

3. We will learn how to predict the phases of the moon.

4. We will study how to parse a sentence.

5. We will review the nerve signaling process.

6. Students will learn how to detect negative framing in political discourse.

7. Students will be able to explain how swamps are formed.

8. We will study the works of Neil Simon.

9. We will cover the Neutrino.

And as a Review of This Chapter

1. The function of objectives in education traditionally has focused on organizing content for teaching.

2. Learning objectives focus on learner competence related to specific content concepts.

3. Learning objectives always have an active verb; implying that the learner is actively involved in the learning process.

4. There are always four components found in a learning objective. The components are:

    • A description of the content (task(s)) to be studied.

    • A description of the conditions required for demonstrating learning.

    • A description of the performance required in order to evaluate competence.

    • A description of the criteria (standard) to be achieved in order to be considered competent.

Chapter Four – The 15-Minute Lecture and its Enrichment

Chapter four objectives – relating to goals 2 & 3 of the book

- By the end of chapter three the reader will be able to competently explain how lecturing can be enhanced to provide for more effective and efficient teaching.

- By the end of chapter three the reader will be able to competently describe how the 15-minute lecture model provides for more effective and efficient teaching.

- By the end of chapter three the reader will be able to competently describe three different teaching enhancement activities and how they reinforce the lecture content to provide for more effective and efficient teaching.

Introduction

In this chapter we will focus on step four of the Wheel for Effective and Efficient Teaching. This chapter will help you understand how the 15-minute lecture and its associated lecture enhancement activities provide for more in-depth learning and better recall – hence – more effective and efficient teaching.

Considering the lecture as a teaching modality

In my experience, new assistant professors or lecturers typically find that the majority of their time is spent preparing and lecturing, yet their personal preparation in how to design and deliver the teaching experience is woefully inadequate, if indeed they have had any instruction in the art of teaching at all. Furthermore, how to help students move abstract concepts into long term memory is like a pure vacuum. Tradition takes over and new instructors, for the lack of any other model, attempt to perform as one or more of their favorite teachers in higher education performed. A Person who, in fact, had no training in the art of teaching and had modeled his/her teacher and the cycle continues. (3).

Lecturing is an ancient art. In my education; I have experienced many kinds, some good and way too many terrible! Many were disorganized, many were very dull, and many did not have much concern about student learning. However all instructors were very bright, and had an excellent handle on the subject they were supposed to be teaching. Never-the-less, I learned most of my "stuff" by reading a lot, writing a lot, having good discussions with my fellow students, and serving as graduate student instructor. Also, I was privileged to have had an excellent advisor during my undergraduate practice teaching semester, who taught me how to learn.

Since I did not considered myself a quality lecturer, over time I began to teach by using a short lecture followed by a learning re-enforcement activity of some sort. During this time I also became interested in teaching for student growth and teaching concepts rather than just factual information. Competence and competence measurement is an added outgrowth of this effort as was the learner-based course objective. All of this became the 15-minute lecture as my files became filled with different types of enrichment activities and strategies for measuring competence.

Introducing the 15-Minute Lecture

When I had an opportunity to work with higher education faculty as a development officer, I attempted to help - those who needed help - change their habits and had some success, but not as much as I would have liked. Over 85 percent of the faculty I worked with taught by use of the 50-minute lecture. Their focus was completely on the lecture pouring a vast amount of knowledge into the eyes and ears of students and not caring too much about student overload and attention span.

The content of the 15-minute lecture can focus on many things. Generally, you might start by identifying 1 or more sub-sub (teaching) concepts related to a course objective and your lecture will focus on stating the teaching concept, expanding on the detail of the concept, suggesting additional readings, etc. and then repeating the teaching concept. Try not to run over 20 minutes unless a dialogue develops between you and your students during your lecture. If so – fine. The subsequent Socratic-type questioning instead of the lecture will serve for the enrichment project for that particular session. This likely would be a very rare happening at least until students are comfortable with questioning.

When using the 15-minute lecture model, I have found that using a 3 part system in which I state what the teaching concept is, then discuss the teaching concept, and then repeat the statement of the teaching concept. This seemed to help my students recall more information after a period of time, but I have no real double-blind research data to prove this. However, the process does follow the principles of the Teaching Continuum and there is considerable evidence of its effectiveness. Of importance is an experimental course that I taught in Critical Thinking, using the principles of the Teaching Continuum, that produced very positive results. I think this may have happened because the students were able to make more extensive notes and doing so reinforced their memories, which clearly sets a frame for any teaching enhancement activity. In any case, the students commonly said that the strategy was helpful. Of course, this hypothesis of mine needs significant research.

Of note, and a bit to the side, I wish to comment on the ubiquitous use of the PowerPoint presentation; which incidentally works well in the 15-minute lecture followed by related activities if you have the specific slide showing the concept during the enrichment activity. PowerPoint presentations provide additional sensory data to be added to the working memory and then to the long-term memory. However, I have often observed them being used incorrectly, mainly as a blackboard in which the teacher reads the statement on a slide aloud and then goes to the next one, reads it aloud, etc. **DON'T DO IT!** It is insulting to the students who, at this stage of their life, are actually pretty good readers. In this case the teacher gives the act of teaching over to the PowerPoint presentation, and has abdicated his/her throne-so to speak. The PowerPoint presentation is best used as a vehicle for stating the major concepts involved in the lesson and the teacher should expand on the concept. Also, do not "gussy up" the slides too much, it is distracting and makes the content of a slide seem less important. (Of course, if you are doing a 50-minute or more lecture, a few jokes here and there might be a beneficial break). I have found that providing students with a paper copy of a PowerPoint presentation, so they can add notes to the paper, is helpful to student learning and recall.

More 15-minute lecture tips

When thinking about your course, consider how you learned and remember the material you will be covering, not on the way you were taught, but how you actually learned the material. Then try to help the student learn the material in much the same way as you did.

Start with the easy stuff and work into the more complex.

ALWAYS start your classes by talking about the lesson's objectives for the day and **ALWAYS** have daily objectives!

If there is a podium in your classroom or anything else you can stand behind – **DON'T DO IT!** Use it for temporary storage or just ignore it. If you need cue cards, or its equivalent, buy a clip-board and carry it with you as you move around the room. And, you should move around the room.

Don't mumble! Students will never forgive that. They will forgive a lot of other things over time even poor organization.

When you are talking, focus your eyes on a section of the room for a minute or so, then move your eyesight to a different part of the room and keep this up during your lecture. Make certain that you do not favor one section of the room as you may lose the students in the other sections. If a question is asked, keep your eyes on the asker.

If a question is asked and you find that you do not have the 'foggiest', say so, but that you will research it and report on it during the next lesson (this assumes that the question was related to the subject – if not, ask **why** the student asked the question). If you really want to be brave, ask if anyone else in the room can answer the question. Or, you might ask the asker what he knows about the issue and then have a short Socratic moment in your lesson.

If you are going to try the Teaching Continuum model and you are new at the business, I recommend that you ease into the process. I suggest that you start by changing your goals and teaching objectives (steps two and three of the wheel), and until you become comfortable with your subject, start your lessons with a ½ hour lecture and then add a dyad model activity as they are generally shorter and connect most easily with the subject.

ALWAYS start and end your lessons on time! Do not wait for students to arrive and do nothing to help them catch up. They will soon be on time and will use other students to catch up – which is beneficial for both of them. Speaking of time; for your first few times doing an enrichment activity, you will have trouble getting students started and ending their discussion. Your time is valuable and you will need to manage the time carefully. In doing so, your students will quickly learn what activities are all about and when to shut-up and get started. MAKE CERTAIN THAT YOUR INSTRUCTIONS ARE CLEAR AND CONCISE!

ALWAYS end your session with a summary or ask one or more of your students to summarize!

You might ask yourself; "how does subject information best go from me to the memory banks of learners?" First of all, it must be seen as important to the learner. A written or unwritten objective of every teacher must be to convince the learner that the "pearls" of wisdom spoken, viewed, listened to, or absorbed in some way, has meaning in their current life. Chances are, what the teacher believes to be inherently interesting will not automatically have the same interpretation by the learner. The teacher will need to convince them and that is part of good teaching. Remember; Learning is not a spectator sport!

Secondly, and requiring a great deal of time and effort on the part of the teacher, is the design that describes how the teaching process is organized. The Teaching Continuum design is where the "rubber-hits-the-road" so to speak and this is where good and poor teaching starts to be separated. Using the continuum, teaching must be aligned in five steps, which are: 1) the purpose of the course, 2) the goals of the course, 3) the learning objectives for the course, 4) the teaching activities, and 5) competence evaluation.

Student learning is less effective when students sit inertly in classes listening to teachers, passively viewing PowerPoint presentations, etc. Students do not remember much just sitting in classes listening to teachers, memorizing prepackaged assignments and spitting out answers. Students must *talk* about what they are learning, *write* about it, *relate* it to past experience, and *apply* it in their own lives. They must make what they learn part of them as this is how the human brain works. Herbert states: "One learns from books only that certain things can be done. Actual learning requires you to do these things." (16)

Most lecturers are comfortable filling the entire lecture hour with words. However, a great deal of research indicates that, for most students, attention begins to diminish after 10-15 minutes into the lecture and the glaze-eye syndrome takes over after 20 minutes. Once they realize that this is relatively ineffective for most students, they do not know how to structure breaks in their lesson. Breaks and mini-lectures are known to enhance memories and should build on and reinforce each other. Successful breaks do not occur spontaneously; they must be planned and scripted. Breaks should clearly shift gears from the lecture to revive student attention for the next mini lecture. Breaks are also more effective when they are varied. The brain easily goes into over-load when it attempts to learn too much material the same way in a short period of time and the breaks positively address the over-load issue.

Try the 15-minute lecture model and its enrichment activities for your teaching design because it is a proven enhancer of learning and provides more effective and efficient teaching. This is because it more closely follows the principles of thinking and memory functions of the human brain than does the traditional 50-minute lecture.

Enrichment Teaching Activities

The function of enrichment teaching activities is to provide more "ways" for the brain to use when storing or recalling memories. Each enrichment activity requires some action on the part of the learner. Each action contains many different sensations provided by the different sense organs involved in the action. Each different sensation is stored in a different part of the brain, which altogether results in long-term memories. The action or actions experienced during an enhancement activity can be more easily recalled because enhancement provides for hundreds or even thousands more handles available in the brain to trigger the recall. This is a part of the "use it or lose it" mechanism of the human brain. Enhancement teaching activities are sometimes referred to as "breaks."

Breaks using groups of two or three (dyads or triads) students per group

1. Instruction to students: For groups of two: "Turn to the student on your right (if in rows, otherwise have students pick their partner) who will be your working partner. Those at the end of a row will need to work with another "loner".

Groups of three can be quickly formed by taking the first three on a row as one group, the second three to be another group etc.

Note 1: I have found that groups larger than three makes this type of break rather clumsy and I use groups larger than three as typical "small group" facilitating.

2. Tell each student their task is to describe to the other(s) what idea presented in the lecture was the most important idea for

the lecture and why she/he thinks so. When one is finished, the next partner describes his/her idea, etc.

Note 2: It is OK for all to have the same idea, but the "whys" might be different.

3. Tell students that they have 5 minutes to complete the task. (Use a stop watch if possible).

4. Tell students that they may be asked to share their idea, and the "why" with the class after the five minutes are up.

Note 3: I have found that it is helpful to move around the room supporting the groups' conversations as the students work. Be definite on the times constraint, particularly when first doing this as students need to understand that you are serious.

5. At the end of the 5 minutes ask one or more groups to share their ideas with the class explaining the "why" in each case. At this point you may question them, but do not evaluate their ideas – save this for the summary at the end of the activity.

Note 4: Absolutely, Positively, **DO NOT** give students a grade for their work in an enhancement activity – it **KILLS IT!**

6. When the first group is finished ask the class "how many have listed the same or close to the same idea?"

7. Depending on available time, ask students who have different ideas to share theirs – be sure that they explain the "why"!

Always manage to save some time for your summary of the activity (occasionally, you might ask a student to summarize). The summary should focus on the lecture; what you had intended, what the student might research, any reading assignment that might be helpful for more in-depth learning, etc.

Note 5: In the beginning, you will find that the 15-minute lecture, the enhancement activity, and your summary will take the full 50-minutes of your class. However, as students become trained in this process, and realize that you are serious, you will find extra time at the end of the session. Be prepared for an extended summary that might segue into a short Socratic discussion.

Other direction questions that you may use in student groups of 2 or 3 are:

- Ask students to relate the lecture to the previous lecture.

- Provide a question along with an answer. Ask the students to explain why the answer is correct or how it has to change to be correct.

- Ask the students to use their own words to explain a concept covered in the lecture.

- Ask the students to generate one or two real world examples of a concept covered in the lecture.

- Ask the students to generate one question that they believe has not been covered in the lecture.

Be creative with your directions. There should be several others not listed above.

Other break ideas

Use a true-false quiz as a review of previous lessons – Make all the question true questions. Ask students to mark "T" If they believe they could correctly answer the question/statement and to mark "F" if they could not. Then, when all are finished, provide the students with the correct answer for all. This will give them an idea of where they need to study.

Run a brainstorming session either in small groups (5 or more) or using the entire class. Follow the rules of brainstorming: no criticizing, building on other's ideas, and use of a recorder, then have students rate the "importance" relative to the question or statement that you posed for the brainstorming session. Compile the results for all groups and discuss.

A one minute paper – Ask students to briefly write out a response to two questions. The questions are: What is the most important thing that you learned in the 15-minute lecture? And, "What issue in the 15-minute lecture is not well understood?

Additional examples of break activities are located in appendix E.

There may be times that you might wish to skip the 15-minute lecture and focus on a system of introducing a problem related to an objective and use small groups of 5-7 students each, to solve the problem. Following are two examples of small group techniques. As with breaks, more small group activities and be found in the appendices.

Small group techniques generally used with groups of five or more.

Cooperative Technique

This technique is structured around a series of 1-1 team building techniques. The instructor assigns a common topic to all teams (groups of 5-7 students) within a class and identifies a series of sub-topics related to the main topic. Each student within a team selects one of the sub-topics, researches it, and shares her/his findings with other members of the team. After team discussion, the information is compiled into a group presentation which is given to the entire class.

Another Cooperative Technique

This technique is similar to the cooperative squared technique, except that each student in the class is assigned a sub-topic by the instructor. The student researches the sub-topic and comes back to class to discuss the sub-topic with other students in class who are engaged in the same sub-topic. Team members then go back to their original team and share their revised response with the team.

One important note: student research is a very important component of teaching. To augment your teaching using the 15-minute model, it is important that you reference readings that relate to specific concepts covered in each lecture. In addition, it would be helpful for student learning to occasionally assign, to groups of 3-5 students, a project to research and provide a group report on some one or more of the concepts covered in a lecture. If you do this, make certain that the groups have enough class time to initially discuss and organize.

And as a Review

1. Learning is NOT a spectator sport!

2. After 15-20 minutes of steady lecturing the average student is not learning.

3. The 15-minute lecture must focus on the concept or concepts involved in the course objectives.

4. It is important that the 15-minute lecture be packaged and delivered using good organization and delivery techniques.

5. Enrichment breaks help the brain develop more enriched long-term memories, which results in greater in-depth leaning and better recall.

6. Enrichment activities must always involve the learner with active (physical and/or mental) learning opportunities.

7. The 15-minute lecture model requires active management of class time.

Chapter five – Student competency evaluation

You will find that the student evaluation process is either the most difficult process or the easiest process for you to adapt to by using the Teaching Continuum model for your teaching design. This is because the continuum focuses on teaching at the conceptual level that requires the use of active verbs in your learning objectives. The student evaluation process is easier because you design the process as a part of the learning objective and it is harder because the active verbs require competency evaluation which cannot be measured by traditional score-based grading systems. This requires you to become familiar with evaluation strategies for which you may not be prepared. This chapter will provide some guidance to help you with this change.

Chapter five objectives relating to goal three of the book

- By the end of this chapter the reader will be able to competently describe how to design a competency based student evaluation process using the principles of the Teaching Continuum as a basis for the design.

Introduction

In chapter four you studied the 15-minute lecture model of teaching, which is step two of the Wheel of Effective and Efficient teaching. In this chapter, you will review student evaluation, which is step three of the wheel. In a perfect world, one could argue that step three is redundant in the Teaching Continuum as formative student evaluation is adequately covered as a part of a learning objective. However, the world is not perfect and the tradition that there must be a separate summative evaluation process dies hard. This chapter will cover processes for measuring concept level thinking skills, which are required when working with competence. This chapter will help teachers conform to an institutional requirement for mid-terms and finals.

The Teaching Continuum Model implies that student evaluation results in one being competent or not. There are no grade scores. However, based on the competency continuum discussed in this chapter, most authors understand that one can become more than competent. I suspect that this could be morphed into a grading scale, but to my knowledge this has not been done and there is no good reason for it to be done other than tradition requires a range of scores. Certainly a good score is not a valid measurement of individual competence and being competent is the standard used to certify adequacy of skills. The Competency Continuum discussed later on in this chapter provides an explanation of this concept.

Competence and Competencies

Over the years, competence has taken a beating relative to its meaning. Many different definitions are found in the literature; many of which have strayed far away from its original meaning. This is particularly true in the case of professional, business, and law schools where competencies are often defined as a list of skills or a set of skills that make up a long list of activities specific to the trade. This is a clear obfuscation of the term competency. Perhaps this problem has its genesis in a dictionary definition of competency. The American Heritage Dictionary, 4th ed., defines competency as having two different meanings:

1. "The state of being competent. i.e. A student has achieved the required level of skill or ability to use the skill."

2. 'A specific **range** of skills, knowledge, or ability." (1)

Other dictionaries do not include number two above. For clarity, further discussion in this book will use the definition stated in number one above to develop the following competence statement: "**Competence is the point on the competency growth continuum in which the learner uses higher level thinking skills to act on the required skills at an agreed upon minimal level of performance as judged by competent professionals in a subject or field of study.**"

The concept of competence had its beginnings in the manufacturing world of business in the early 1900s, when competence was thought to better measure the total production quality of workers in the industries; actually as part of the time-management epoch. This movement was eventually adopted by technical and vocational schools where the outcomes of competence are more easily identified and assessed. Today the competency movement has progressed, albeit slowly, into accrediting agencies and schools that offer professional training of various sorts; unfortunately often inappropriately focusing on knowledge of facts and other detail, instead of concepts.

In the 1960s David McClelland (7) proposed a view that segued the competency movement away from focusing completely on knowledge, to skills and attitudes that focus more on the skills that are found to consistently distinguish outstanding from minimal performance in a given job or role. It should be noted that different competencies predict outstanding performance in different roles, and that there is a limited number of competencies that predict outstanding performance in any given job or role. Thus, a trait that is a 'competence' for one job might not predict outstanding performance in a different role. Competence is specific to situation. McClelland's ideas form the basis for the continuing development of competency measurement strategies. McClelland also argues that competencies can neither be identified nor assessed using traditional assessment procedures. Competencies such as these cannot be assessed by way of the processes favored by traditional psychometricians.

Lately the idea of competence has often been reduced to a list of discrete activities, in which people are thought to possess the necessary skills, knowledge and understanding to engage in a skill effectively. The implication here is that behavior can be objectively and mechanistically measured. This is a highly questionable assumption as there always has to be some uncertainty about what is being measured. It is often very difficult to judge what the impact of particular experiences has been. Sometimes it is years after an event that we come to appreciate something of what has happened. Yet, there is something more. In order to measure mechanistically, things have to be broken down into smaller and smaller units. The result is a long list of trivial skills labeled "Competencies" that is frequently encountered in professional schools. This can lead to a focus on parts rather than the whole; on the trivial, rather than the significant. It can lead to an approach to education and assessment which resembles a shopping list. When all the items are ticked, the person has passed. Or worse yet, because of the size of the list, the multiple choice format is used to obtain a score. In both cases the focus is on the score and not on actual competence. McClelland indicates that no more than 12 competencies are needed to encompass the range of a human skill.

The Competency Continuum

Broudy posits a competency continuum based on the increasing use of knowledge that moves from associative, to replicative, to applicative, and ends with interpretive competence levels contrasted against degrees of competence to form a matrix. The continuum starts with novice and goes to competent to expert and ends with grand master. The skill degrees listed in the continuum matrix below are measures of learner growth, which are cumulative and illustrate a developmental aspect as one moves from the left to the right of the matrix. (4)(Refer to matrix on page 57).

Consideration of the behaviors, as applied to historical evaluation efforts, makes one aware of considerable incongruence related to the measurement of competency. In professional schools, competency is generally assessed at the associative level, attested to by the preponderance of tests focusing on recognition and/or recall. I have found, along with common opinion of other researchers, that competency is more validly measured at the replicative degree. Competent behaviors, at the replicative level, are associated with such things as the specific situation in which the behaviors are observed, the idiosyncratic characteristics of the evaluatee, etc.; thus, unique to the situation. (14)

According to the matrix the levels of knowledge development are directly related to the degree of learner development. The lowest level of learner development – novice - is referred to as the associative level of knowledge development. Competency is referred to as the replicative level. Expert is referred to as the applicative level. And the highest degree of skill development is called the "grand master" and is associated with the interpretive level of skill development. Competence is generally regarded, particularly in the professions, as the required level of professional skills or the minimal requirements for practicing an art and/or science such as teaching. (14)

TABLE 1 Knowledge Matrix

Knowledge Level	Degree of skill			
	Novice	Competent	Expert	Grand Master
Associative	Behaviors that identify meaning of words/ concepts			
Replicative		**Behaviors that can be called into action and be replicated precisely. Higher level thinking skills are used**		
Applicative			Behaviors that are based on principles and theory of great generality and are altered for new situations	
Interpretive				Behaviors based on evaluative "maps" with solid perceptual structures that mark out new realities and create new concepts

Competency evaluation

When we add the requirement that in order to be considered competent one must exhibit higher level thinking, the evaluation problem becomes more complex as much of the traditional student evaluation processes become obsolete. This requires one to do some in-depth soul-searching in order to accomplish the student evaluation of competence in a valid and reliable way. Thankfully, over the years many people have been studiously developing just such techniques and are available to us for direct or modified use. The 15-minute lecture course model in chapter six provides one example of formative student competency evaluation suggested by the learning objectives, coupled by a non-competitive process using similar strategies for summative evaluation design.

Any evaluation process needs a focus and evaluating competence is no exception. Competency evaluation focuses on measuring the higher level learning skills associated with competence. In addition, competence is unique to an individual student and because of this, traditional methods of measuring knowledge growth does not work. Competency evaluation entails different methodologies that occupy more time, and a non-competitive focus. It is uniquely personal to the student and because of this it makes a lot of sense to include it in the learning process rather than by way of competitive exams and finals. This is the main reason why the learning objective, as defined in this book, is used in the Teaching Continuum and is illustrated in chapter six as part of the weekly activities. (Note that mid-term and final activities are also included in the chapter six model as an add-on for institutions that require such archaic processes).

Learning objectives require a demonstration of a skill or skills at a defined level and once that is achieved no further evaluation is necessary, unless of course one wants to become an expert or a grand-master, both of which require a more complicated and costly evaluation process. The use of learning objectives obviates the necessity for finals and midterms as competence is addressed in the learning process.

A unique process for on-going formative/summative evaluation of competence is discussed by Faucher and Laberge. They approached evaluating competency of nursing students by first defining Key Learning and Evaluation Objects (KLO) for the course, which are statements similar to competencies. "The KLOs were made operational by 1) taking into account the nature of the KLO, 2) with a view to a progressive mastery of the learning leading to integration, 3) by integrating a formative process that makes ample use of feedback, and 4) by developing an evaluation plan that gives the student more than one occasion to demonstrate what they have learned". (13)

The rubric that was developed for planning and scoring was an individualized matrix with the KLOs listed vertically and the evaluation experiences listed horizontally. In their work they provided scoring points (including an R which meant retake) that, in the end, needed to add up to 100 in order for the student to be deemed competent. Using the rubric, the student would know where they stood on a daily basis and this would be instrumental in helping the student take charge of their own learning. (13)

Competence Evaluation Strategies

Evaluation strategies that have been successfully used by various institutions to measure competence are:

- Direct observation or shadowing

- Standardized oral examinations

- Objective standardized examinations

- Simulations or models

- Chart-stimulated recall

- Global rating

- 360 degree evaluation

- Portfolios

- Record review

- Others, but not limited to, written examinations, surveys, procedure logs, case–based modules, and many more, which in general can be used for formative and summative purposes.

Brief descriptions of the above evaluation strategies follows

Direct observation or shadowing – Some version of the faculty member observing the behavior of the student while performing the skill or evaluating a student's written or oral product.

Standardized oral examinations – Typically requires the student to review a case or solve a case in the presence of a faculty member and orally describe the thought processes involved in doing the task.

Objective standardized exam – such as mini-quizzes or computerized modules combining both education and evaluation. For competencies use the essay or modified essay format.[2]

Simulations and modules – can be useful in evaluating procedural skills.

Chart stimulated recall – this provides an opportunity for the student to verbally review processes and procedures needed to demonstrate a skill. It is most often used in health care training institutions.

Global rating – this requires the learner to judge a competency as a category rather than evaluating specific behaviors, skills or tasks. Problems involved with this rubric include maintaining objectivity and reliability.

Portfolios – This is a defined set of materials collected by the student reflecting on performances. Carefully established criteria are important as guidelines for self-reporting competence. This is very time-consuming for both the learner and the teacher.

Record review – This involves trained staff using standardized coding to abstract information for written records. This is particularly successful when used to evaluate competencies related to procedures and planning.

Assessment of Competence

Assessment links student performance to specific learning outcomes in order to provide useful feedback to the teacher about how successfully students are meeting the outcomes expected by the teacher. Grades are a measure of student achievement at the novice level; however, there are significant drawbacks to using grades as indicators of competence.

---

2   See appendix A for styles of modified essay questions. There are other MEQ styles.

Traditional grading which offers one score does not represent student's performance on a whole host of outcomes and does not provide the teacher with detailed and specific information specific to the objectives of a course. This is because grades do not tell the teacher about student performance on individual learning goals or outcomes; they provide little information on the overall success of a course in helping students attain the specific and distinct learning objectives of interest and they are not linked to long-term memory enhancement.

Linking assessment of competence with teaching makes the learning process more effective and consistent by systematically linking student performance to improvement. This is why doing assessment as part of the teaching act is so effective. Classroom assessment makes the learning process more effective and consistent by systematically linking assignments, course structure and assessment practices to intended learning objectives, helps teachers become better teachers by offering specific feedback on what is working and what is not working, and provides systematic feedback to students about their own progress. (14)

One of the guiding principles of student evaluation is that the way you assess students should reflect as close as possible with what you want them to learn. If you want to check whether or not they have acquired content detail, you might use something like a paper-and-pencil test that requires them to display that lower level of learning. But if you want them to be able to construct an argument, resolve a problem, drive a car, sew a button, defend an opinion, etc., then you use an assessment technique that measures competence. This implies evaluation processes that focus on analytical, synthesis, and/or judging levels of thinking. This means the use of learning objectives, as described in this book, in a teaching design that helps the teacher focus on individual students, which aids in being a more effective and efficient teacher.

Student Evaluation

If institutional policy permits, I would prefer using the same type of small group processes that would be used during a course to judge student competence. The final exam would be a take-home, open-book examination. Students would choose a set of three problems from a given list at the end of week 14 and be told to work on the problems at home or at school, and bring their report to the 15th week time slotted for finals.

During this session, they will work on their problems in dyad groups to make suggestions for any changes needed in each student report. Individual students will then write about the accuracy of their report; what changes were made in class and why they were made. Students would be given an extra week to write up their report if they so desire. This would be a P/F grade as judged by the instructor.

This is clearly not a traditional final examination. However, it supports the concept of the learning objective as it focuses on student competence, dealing with individual competence and not student to student competition as measured by a meaningless, (relative to competence) normed score. Students would be deemed competent only if they are able to demonstrate the outcomes established in the goals and learning objectives and demonstrate the level of quality established by the learning objective criteria.

As a Review

1. Evaluating competence, for most teachers, schools and agencies, requires a 180 degree change from traditional student evaluation processes.

2. There are many tried and true teaching and evaluating strategies available for teaching and evaluating competence.

3. Traditional test scores cannot be validly used to ascertain individual competence.

4. This chapter posits a competency continuum with four levels: novice, competent, expert, and grand-master.

5. Competent is the second step on the competency continuum. Higher levels of skill development are possible.

6. Competence is validly assessed by using procedures requiring higher level of thinking skills on the part of students.

7. Competitive-based test scores do not validly measure competence or higher level competency skills. However, such tests may be used to measure novice level skills.

Chapter Six - A model teaching design for you – Critical Reasoning 101

I have designed a course following the principles of the Teaching Continuum and the Wheel for Effective and Efficient Teaching. It was designed to provide a model that you might follow if you decide to use the Teaching Continuum model in your teaching efforts. I had no experience teaching about how to think critically when I originally designed the course – so I decided to teach it. Which I did! I found some needed changes and found that the model actually works. My students did show considerable growth according to a commercial critical thinking test, pre and post, all met the learning objectives, and best of all they continually rated the course high. All together, it was a success. However, it was a course for no credit and that might make a difference. I suggest you give it a try and find out.

Chapter Six Objective – relating to goals 1-3 of the book

- By the end of this chapter the reader will be able to competently evaluate a course that has been designed to follow the principles found in the Teaching Continuum and the Wheel for Effective and Efficient Teaching.

Introduction

I originally labeled this course "Critical Thinking 99," but after teaching it I decided that the label critical thinking was a cliché that everyone thought differently about. This confused the students, so I changed "thinking" to "reasoning," which, in my language, means the same thing. Also, now that I have had experience teaching it, I raised the number from 99 to 101. All of which is probably something that does not interest you.

I have chosen the lecture method for this model design as it is the most commonly used method of teaching in higher education and I think that the lecture process can be enhanced to produce students with a better understanding of subject matter and with longer and more enriched memories. That being said, I am not particularly keen on the use of the 50-minute, traditional lecture and early on in my rather lengthy career, I began to modify the experience.

My bias on lecturing is best described by Richard Paul in a part of his book dealing with didactic vs. dialogical or dialectical thinking. He states: "Didactic thinking encourages monological thinking from beginning to end. There is little room for dialogical or dialectical thinking in the mind of a didactic teacher. Rather, the teacher usually focuses on content coverage, tells students directly what to believe and think about subject matter, while students, in turn, focus on remembering what the teacher said in order to reproduce it on demand. In its most common form, this mode of teaching falsely assumes that one can directly give a person knowledge without that person having to think his or her way to it, and that knowledge can directly be implanted into a student's mind through memorization." (5) I believe that learning is an active process.

This course is designed as in introductory course to critical reasoning. The content of the course will primarily focus on three major components of critical reasoning, which are premises, inferences, and assumptions. Other components such as framing, pseudo-reasoning, and listening will be introduced.

General Information on Class Structure

There are 3, 50-minute daily sessions each week which corresponds to a traditional 3 semester credit course. For this model course, each of the 50 minutes will have a 15-minute lecture, which will concentrate on the concepts related to the weekly learning activities. The lecture will be followed by a 20-minute enrichment activity that requires students to be actively engaged in learning more about the weekly concepts. This is followed by a group discussion related to the lecture and enrichment concepts. This period may be a summary of the day's activities and occasionally a time for personal evaluation for students. Occasionally, the lecture component may be dropped completely. This daily model will be used for 13 of the 15 weeks with the other two weeks saved for midterm and final student evaluation activities. For summative evaluation, students may choose to receive a letter grade based on the pass-fail problem-solving system used in daily lessons, or they may choose to receive a letter grade based on the competitive scores of a paper exam. All written exams will contain essay questions and/or modified essay questions.

The following model of Critical Reasoning will be used in this course:

Critical Reasoning is a type of thinking in which thinkers improve the quality of their reasoning by carefully analyzing the premises and inferences used when making decisions as well as the influences of their personal, situational, and social biases on assumptions used when making those decisions.

The Model Course

CRITICAL REASONING 101
LEARNING HOW TO USE
CRITICAL REASONING IN DAILY LIFE
PURPOSE OF THE COURSE

One focus of professional education is the development of judgment skills. This course will frame critical reasoning as a main component of quality problem solving with a focus on personal judgment skills. It will use the identified model of critical reasoning, which like all good thinking models, contains the notion that good judgment is the assessing of information, the validity of that information, and good self-judgment that looks at the self-bias involved. Much of this course is designed to help students understand, define, and practice the components of critical reasoning, which are premises, inferences, assumptions, and personal or social biases. This course has no prerequisites, but builds on the decision-making skills that students bring to class. It should be considered as a starting course in critical reasoning

Note: I really wrestled with the course purpose. My internal argument related to the inclination to make the purpose longer by adding a little more detail about critical reasoning, but, in the end I did not as I know how committees operate. The committee discussion process would undoubtedly add detail to the statement and in the end, would make it longer and likely inhibit the freedom that the teacher might need in order to provide adjustments during the semester.

COURSE GOALS

1. At the end of the course the students will be able

to competently use the stated components of critical thinking skills when solving a given problem.

2. At the end of the course the students will be able to competently describe their personal biases having an impact on assumptions made when solving a problem.

Note: My first draft of this described 6 goals and counting. Eventually, I came to understand that the two above adequately covered all 6 of them. As is, they are large concepts of what I think students should know about critical thinking at the end of the course that they did not know at the beginning. I used a lot of paper making lists, consulting lists and modifying lists before I began to better understand that the goals needed to be a large picture concept. In this case, one picture with two frames is all that is needed – at least for me.

COURSE OBJECTIVES

1. At the end of the course the student, when given a problem, will be able to identify, describe, and evaluate assumptions used while solving a problem.

2. At the end of the course the student, when given a problem, will be able to identify, describe, and evaluate inferences used while solving a problem.

3. At the end of the course the student, when given a problem, will be able to identify, describe, and evaluate premises used while solving a problem.

4. 4. At the end of the course the student, when given a problem, will be able to identify and describe personal or social biases that have an impact on assumptions made while solving a problem.

Note: My first effort for defining the learning objectives for this critical reasoning course was a complete flop as I started by using way too much detail. When my list of objectives reached eight, I needed to rethink my strategy. After many efforts I discovered that many I had written were actually teaching activity objectives and I revised the list to the ones above. I am a big picture person who has trouble with detail, yet, too much detail was my major problem with this step as with the prior one. It was much easier, even with my big picture style, to compose detail than it was to think in conceptual terms (see what education can do to one's natural behaviors!). Comparing lists and looking for congruousness helped. Since teachers fit at various points on the detail – big picture continuum, the difficulty conceiving objectives as concepts will likely vary considerably among individuals. I suspect, more so for those who happen to prefer detail. Obviously, I am making an assumption that if a student is competent in the two goals, he/she is competent in critical reasoning, but there are considerable reasoning concepts to learn beyond this effort.

COURSE TEACHING ACTIVITIES

I will present the course activities as a weekly schedule; showing the week number, the title of the weekly activity, the course and teaching objectives for each weekly activity, the problem to be worked on and any supportive documentation that the students may use in their group discussion. Each week will approximately follow the weekly procedure of: a mini-lecture, followed by a break for an enrichment activity, or may include other activities such as student as teacher, student-to-student concept clarification, teacher mini-lecture on problems identified, and other memory reinforcement activities, followed by a review session; ending each session with students evaluating their perceived quality of the session. In the final session of the teaching weeks, the discussion activity will focus on students evaluating their growth in critical reasoning based on the course objectives.

The break activities are designed to promote memory enrichment by repetition, by teaching someone, by explaining something in different ways, by rehearsing, by using concepts in different ways, and changing the environment in which learning occurs. Motivation to learn will be enhanced by: demonstrating intrinsic value of new knowledge, showing relationships to quality of current life, promoting enjoyment while learning, helping the learner take more responsibility for their learning, providing a stress-free learning environment, and enabling the learner to evaluate their own progress. All of the teaching objectives focus on goals one and two of the course.

DEFINITIONS

Assumption - A modifying statement taken for granted that may or may not be true.

Inference – To conclude by reasoning from premises and/or assumptions that may or may not be true.

Premise – A proposition (anything stated for a discussion) supporting a conclusion or argument which may or may not be true.

WEEKLY CALENDAR

Week One – The three sessions will focus on setting the stage for learning. Each session will start with a 15-minute lecture on critical reasoning – briefly what it is and what it not. In the first session students will be involved in an enrichment activity called Rebus Names (29) with the teaching objective of getting acquainted. Students will be asked to take the Cornell Critical Thinking

Test – Level X. (Level Z will be administered at the end of the course in order to provide individual student growth patterns). The objective of the test is to enable students to consider their growth in competence for each course goal and help them identify what they need to learn in order to be considered competent. Another enrichment group activity is called "Is the Earth Hollow". (24) This activity will help students distinguish fact from fiction. A discussion period about critical reasoning and review of the teaching activities for the remaining weeks will complete the first week.

Week two – The 15-Minute lectures and enrichment activities for this week will focus on identifying and evaluating explicit assumptions found in decision statements. The enrichment activities for the week are:

1. A triad cooperative group activity in which explicit assumptions will be identified in given decision statements

2. A triad cooperative group activity called "Examining Assumptions," (29) in which students in triad groups will work on evaluating explicit assumptions

3. A triad cooperative group activity in which students will work on correcting invalid explicit assumptions that they have identified. The follow-up discussion session will review concepts covered this week and introduce the concepts that will be covered next week

These activities are designed to develop student's ability to distinguish between types of assumptions in analyzing information.

Week 3 - The 15-minute lectures and enrichment activities will focus on the concepts of the implicit assumption; how to identify implicit assumptions found, or implied, in decision statements and the personal belief systems associated with the assumptions. The enrichment activities for this week are:

1. A triad cooperative group activity engaging students in the identification of implicit (hidden) assumptions in a list of decision statements

2. A triad group activity called: "Taking Responsibility – Practice in Communicating Assumptions" (28) in which students practice identifying personal assumptions

3. A dyad group experience in which students will discover the difficulties inherent in assumptions found in verbal decision statements

The activities are designed to help students develop their abilities to identify, evaluate, and correct implicit assumptions and be introduced to the relationships between personal beliefs and assumptions. The follow-up discussion session will review concepts covered this week and introduce the concepts that will be covered next week.

Week 4 - The 15-minute lectures and enrichment activities for this week will focus on the concepts related to personal belief and value systems and their impact on the quality of explicit and implicit assumptions. The enrichment activities for the week are:

1. A full group class review of concepts covered in the prior three weeks

2. A dyad cooperative group activity in which students are introduced to personal values

3. Cooperative groups of five will be involved in an activity called the Values Clarification Instrument. (29)

The teaching activities are designed to further develop student knowledge of their personal belief and value systems. The follow-up discussion session will review concepts covered this week and introduce the concepts that will be covered next week.

Week 5 - The 15-minute lectures and enrichment activities for this week will provide an opportunity for students to review the reasoning concepts they have studied and practiced during the previous weeks. Belief and value system influence on assumptions will be studied and practiced. The enrichment activities for the week are:

1. Taking a mock Nearly Perfect Test, which is a true/false test with all the concepts covered in the previous weeks listed – and all are true

2. An enrichment activity called "Personal Value Statement Process" (29) will help students understand their personal value system and will be used for that purpose

3. An enrichment activity called "The Girl and the Sailor: Value Clarification" (29) will provide opportunities for students to evaluate their personal beliefs and values on assumptions identified in decision statements

The follow-up discussion will focus on linking personal beliefs and values with their personal judgments made when evaluating decision statements as well as the concepts covered this week and will introduce the concepts that will be covered next week.

Week 6 - The 15-minute lectures and enrichment activities for this week will focus on identifying, analyzing, evaluating, and correcting non-valid assumptions. The enrichment activities for the week are:

1. Dyad group members will be given a sheet with several decision statements. Their task is to identify

assumptions (both implicit and explicit), judge the validity of each assumption identified, and make corrections for assumptions that are not valid

2. Participate in an activity called "Value System Instrument" (29) which is designed to help learners identify oral-based assumptions

3. Dyad groups will be given a sheet with two decision statements with each member having different statements. One student will read the first statement and the other will identify the assumption. This continues until the four different statements have been evaluated.

The group discussions will focus on the belief and value concepts covered and the difficulties involved with oral evaluations. The follow-up discussion session will also review concepts covered this week and introduce the concepts that will be covered next week.

Week 7 - The 15-minute lectures and enrichment activities for the week will focus on introducing inferences; the part they play in clinical reasoning and how they can be identified and changed. The enrichment activities for the week are:

1. Students, working first individually and then in dyad groups will be given a list of decision statements and asked to identify the assumptions and inferences for each decision statement

2. Students, working in triad groups will be asked to develop two new clinical reasoning statements using valid assumptions and inferences in the new statements

3. Students working in triad groups will be asked to invent two new clinical reasoning statements using valid assumptions and inferences and explain why they are valid.

The follow-up discussion will focus on reviewing the concepts covered during the week and introduce the next week's midterm activities.

Week 8 - This is mid-term week. Basically, this week is a review of reasoning concepts covered in the previous weeks, an opportunity for individual practice to analyze decision statements that will be judged by other students in dyad groups, and will have a short essay on "What I have learned in this course that I did not know or understand prior to the course". The follow-up discussion will review the essays and introduce the concepts that will be covered the following week.

Week 9 - The 15-minute lectures and enrichment activities for this week will focus on inferences and their relationships to the assumptions made when making judgments relative to decision statements. The enrichment activities for the week are:

1. Triad groups will work on an inference activity called "Sherlock: an Inference Activity" (28)

2. An individualized and general activity called "Who Killed Harry Skank?" (24)

3. A 5 member group activity called "Deciphering Euphemisms" (24)

The discussion periods will focus on inference concepts and their relationship to critical reasoning, will review concepts covered this week, and introduce the concepts that will be covered next week.

Week 10 - The 15-minute lectures and enrichment activities for this week will continue to focus on identifying inferences and their inherent assumptions as well as judging the validity of these two parts when given decision statements. The enrichment activities for this week are:

1. A small group activity called "Is the Earth Hollow", (24) an activity designed to evaluate evidence

2. A dyad activity called "From Known to Unknown", (24) an activity designed to help students evaluate how personal biases/values influence inferences

3. A small group activity called "Weighing the Evidence", (24) which is designed to help students determine criteria for effective use of evidence and the importance of judging the reliability of evidence

The follow-up discussion will relate to the concepts covered in the lecture and enrichment activities, focusing mainly of quality judgments of bias in inferences and assumptions and will review concepts covered this week and introduce the concepts that will be covered next week.

Week 11 - The 15-minute lectures and enrichment activities for this week focus on the use of logic in critical reasoning. The validity of the premise or premises made in decision statements will be emphasized. The enrichment activities for this week are:

1. Triad groups will be given a list of decision statements and will work on the solution of problems in each statement using logic

2. A Socratic discussion to be lead by the instructor on the question "When can logic be used to solve the validity of a critical reasoning statement"

3. Dyad groups identifying why and when to use logic when evaluating a list of decision statements. The discussions will relate to the logic concepts covered in the lectures and enrichment activities.

The follow-up discussion session will review concepts

covered this week and introduce the concepts that will be covered next week and the follow-up discussion session will review concepts covered this week and introduce the concepts that will be covered next week.

Week 12 - The 15-minute lectures and enrichment activities for this week focus on the concepts involved in the process of framing and its influence on premises, assumptions, and inferences made in critical reasoning. The enrichment activities for this week are:

1. Students will be given a list of written scenarios and will work in triad groups to identify the framing process used in the scenarios

2. Students, working in the same triad group, will be asked for assumptions and inferences used in the scenarios

3. Students, working in the same triad group will be asked to evaluate, and change if necessary, the assumptions and inferences identified in the previous activity

The follow-up discussion session will focus on the relationships between framing and assumptions and inferences used and how to change the frame focus by changing the assumptions and inferences. Week 13 concepts will be introduced.

Week 13 - The 15-minute lectures and enrichment activities for this week will focus on fallacies (pseudo-reasoning) (see appendix D) and their effect on premises, assumptions, and inferences made in decision statements. The enrichment activities for this week are:

1. When given a list of decision statements and a list of fallacies, students working in dyad groups will identify the fallacies found in the decision statements

2. Students working in the same dyad group will be asked to identify the assumptions found in the fallacies in the prior session

3. Students working in the same dyad group will be asked to evaluate the identified assumptions and re-write the decision statement by changing the assumptions

The follow-up discussion session will review concepts covered this week and introduce the concepts that will be covered the following week.

Week 14 – The 15-minute lectures for this week will focus on listening and its effects on the quality of premises, assumptions, and inferences made in decision statements. Also, the concepts of active listening will be reviewed. This will focus on detecting assumptions and inferences in oral decision statements. The enrichment activities for this week are:

1. Students listen to oral decision statements read by the instructor and identify the rehearsing, judging, identifying, advising, and derailing blocks to active listening in the scenarios

2. Students will work in dyad groups to associate assumptions and inferences related to the blocks to active listening

3. Students, in the same dyad groups as in the previous activity, will be asked to evaluate and change, if necessary, the assumptions and inferences identified in the previous session

The follow-up discussion will focus on reviewing the blocks to active listening and the assumptions and inferences associated with the blocks. Some time will be saved to be used to discuss the final.

Week 15 – This is "finals" week. Since, traditionally, this is a week of no classes and finals are scheduled around two-hour blocks of time, students will be given two options. In one option, students may take a traditional test with modified essay questions to solve. In this option, they will receive a traditional final grade based on their position in the range of scores obtained for the group taking the test. In the second option, they will be given a list of decision statements and will be told to competently analyze them, discussing the validity of the premises, assumptions, and inferences as well as identifying any personal biases or values they used in their judgments. In this option, they will receive a P/F grade and will pass if their analysis is judged competent by the instructor.

Final Notes for the Teaching Continuum and the Wheel of Effective and Efficient Teaching

While developing the activities I found it easy to follow the principle of alignment as this is what I have always done, albeit inadvertently. However, the need for traditional teaching concepts was new to me. I believe that I visualized the need for teaching concepts when dealing with the course objectives and finding it difficult to adjust them to a reasonable concept. By doing this, I was able to complete the learning objective as a larger concept and provided the detail in the weekly teaching objectives. As is, I kind of like the weekly teaching concepts as, in my case, it helped me give a clear pathway for the introductory mini-lectures and aids in student-to-student evaluation activities as they work at practicing critical reasoning.

The format for the activities was taken in part from prior teaching sessions, with some input from the textbooks from which the activities were taken, along with quite a few modifications that were needed in order to better fit the ideas presented in chapters one through five. I found this very time consuming and suspect that there would be many changes suggested after the final review with students at the end of the course – and perhaps during the course itself.

There could be several different ways to provide opportunities for students to rehearse, discuss, teach, and evaluate their learning in addition to the activities presented in this course. Several suggestions have been given in chapter five and a plethora of suggestions can be found through the internet and in the appendices.

One final note, I had used the performance type of objectives for many years. Never-the-less, how I handled the conversion to learning objectives with its standard statement was clumsy at best. To have the statement be concise and clear to the student was sometimes difficult for me to conceptualize. Competencies are skills that are conceptual and made up of several skills operating simultaneously. I fought with the personal need to measure them by the use of traditional, competitive techniques. I spent more time per unit of output (mark this as frustration) during objective writing than I did when writing the teaching activities. Of course, this helped me breeze through the evaluation component of the wheel, and helped me learn more about the business of measuring competence.

BIBLIOGRAPHY

1. American Heritage Dictionary 4thed., Bantam Dell, New York, 2004

2. Biggs, John, "Aligning Teaching and Assessment to Curriculum Objectives", A Paper Published by the Generic Center of Learning and Teaching Network, ITSN, Generic Center.

3. Biggs, John and Catherine Tang, Teaching for Quality Learning at University 3rd ed., Open University Press, Buckingham, England, 2007.

4. Broudy, H. D., Democaracy and Excellence in American Education, Rand McNalley, Chicago, 1967.

5. Budson, Andrew G and Bruce H. Price, "Memory Dysfunction," New England Journal of Medicine, February 17, 2005.

6. "Competence and Competency", Infield Search, www.infed. org.biblio-b-comp. 1967.

7. "Constructivist Learning Theory," www.exploratorium.edu/ ITI/.

8. D'Andrea, Vareeta and David Gosling, Improving Higher Teaching and Learning in Higher Education, McGraw-Hill, Berkshire, England 2005.

9. DeBono, Edward, Six Thinking Hats, Little, Brown, and Company, Boston, 1999

10. Dewey, John, <u>How we Think</u>, Houghton-Mifflin, Boston, 1998.

11. Edelman, Gerald, <u>Brain Science and Human Knowledge</u>, Yale University Press, London, 2006.

12. Faucher, Nicolas and Clement LaBerge, <u>Evaluating Competencies: Theory and Practice</u>, Pedagogie Collegiale, Vol 22, n.1, Fall 2008.

13. Giles, Emory, "Ascertaining Excellence: A State of the Art Message," <u>Journal of Manipulative and Physiological Therapuetics</u>, V. 9, No. 2, Williams & Wilkins, Baltimore, June, 1986.

14. Gross, Ronald, <u>Peak Learning: A Master Course on Learning How to Learn</u>, G. P. Putnam's Sons, New York, 1991.

15. Herbert, Frank, <u>Dune</u>, The Berkley Publishing Group, New York, 1987.

16. Kizlik, Bob, "Definitions of Behavioral Verbs for Learning Objectives," <u>ADPRIMA – Education Information for New and Future Teachers</u>, March 30, 2009.

17. Knowles, Malacom S., Elwood F. Hooten III, and Richard A. Swanson, <u>The Adult Learner 6th ed.</u>, Eloevier, Amsterdam, 2005.

18. Man-ch'ing, Cheng & Robert Smith, <u>Tai Chi</u>, Charles Tuttle Co., Vermont, 1984.

19. McBer, Hay, "Research Into Teaching and Learning in Higher Education", Research Report no. 216, The Crown Copyright Unit, Her Majesty's Stationary Office, Norwich, England, 2005.

20. MedicineNet, "Definition of Short Term Memory," 2009, www.medterms.com/script?/.

21. Merriam, Sharan and Rosemary S. Cafarella, <u>A Master Course on Learning How to Learn 3rd.ed.</u>, Jossey-Bass, San Francisco, 2007.

22. Mesulan, M-Maisel, <u>Principles of Behavioral and Cognitive</u>

Neurology, 2<u>nd</u>. ed., Oxford University Press, New York, 2000.

23. Nelson, John, <u>Cultivating Judgment, A Sourcebook for Teaching Critical Thinking Across the Curriculum</u>, New Forums Press, Stillwater, OK, 2005.

24. Norris, Stephen P. and Robert Ennis, <u>Evaluating Critical Thinking</u>, Critical Thinking Press and Software, California, 1989.

25. Omrod, Jeanne Ellis, <u>Human Learning 2<u>nd</u> ed.</u>, Prentice-Hall, New Jersey, 1995.

26. Paul, Richard W., <u>Critical Thinking: How to Prepare Students for a Rapidly Changing World</u>, Foundation for Critical Thinking, Santa Rosa, CA, 1980.

27. Pfeiffer, William and John Jones, eds., <u>A Handbook of Structured Experiences for Human Relations Training</u>, University Associates, California, Vols. IV and X.

28. Pfeiffer, William, ed., <u>Developing Human Resources : The 1995, 1994, 1989,1985, 1982, and 1977 Annuals</u>, University Associates, California, 1995.

29. Pinel, John P. J., <u>Biophysiology, 5<u>th</u>. Ed.</u>, Allyn & Bacon, Boston, 2003.

30. ReStack, Richard, <u>Mysteries of the Mind</u>, National Geographic Society, Washington DC, 2000.

31. Ruhl, K. L., Hughes, C. A., and Schloss, P.J., "Using the Pause Procedure to Enhance Lecture Recall," <u>Teacher Education and Special Education</u>, 10, 1987, 14-18.

32. Schacter, David, <u>Searching for Memory : The Brain, the Mind, and the Past</u>, Basic Books, New York, 1996.

33. Shors, Tracey J., "Saving New Brain Cells," <u>Scientific American</u>, March 2009, pp. 47 – 52.

34. "Speaking of Memory, An Interview of Eric Kandal by Steve Ayan, <u>Scientific American Mind</u>, November, 2008, p. 16-17.

35. Wankat, Philip C., <u>The Effective and Efficient Professor –
Teaching, Scholarship, and Service</u>, Allyn & Bacon, Boston,
2002.

36. Weimer, Maryellen, <u>Learner Centered Teaching</u>, Jossey-Bass,
San Francisco, 2002.

37. Zull, James E., <u>The Art of Changing the Brain</u>, Stylus
Publishing, Virginia, 2002.

APPENDIX A

Sample of a modified essay question (MEQ) often used in the medical field

Problem:

An unresponsive 58-year-old woman is brought to the emergency department after collapsing at a local shopping mall. Her family reports that she felt well that morning but developed a progressively severe headache. She has had hypertension and arterial fibrillation and is taking an antihypertensive medication and oral anticoagulant. Her blood pressure is 220/130 mm Hg and she has apnea alternating with hyperapnea. She responds only to noxious stimuli with extensor posturing involving the right arm and leg. Funduscopic examination shows papilledema involving the left optic disc. Pupils are 3.0/7.0 (R/L) with no reaction to light on the left. There is a left gaze preference. There is diffuse hyper-reflexia, R.L, and bilalteral Babinski signs are present.

Questions:

1. The dilated, un-reactive left pupil is most consistent with injury to which of the following structures on the left?

A. Optic Nerve

D. Lateral Geniculate Nucleus

B. Optic Tract

E. Superior Colliculus

C. Oculomotor Nerve

2. The extensor posturing on the right is most consistent with injury to which of the following areas of the brain on the left?

   A. Telencephalon   D. Pons

   B. Diencelphalon   E. Medulla

   C. Midbrain

3. Which of the following best describes her respiratory pattern?

   A. Cheyne-Stokes   C. Apneustic

   B. Central neurogenic hyperventilation   D. Ataxic

4. Which one of the following herniation syndromes is most consistent with her clinical presentations?

   A. Cingulate gyrus beneath the falx.

   B. Temporal lobe uncus across the tenotium

   C. Diencephalon through the tenrorial notch

   D. Brain stem through the tentorial notch

   E. Cerebellar tonsils through the foramen mangnum

And the list of questions could go on.

Other examples of MEQs include:

SHORT ANSWER ESSAY:

Sir Isaac Newton has made a great contribution to our understanding of mechanics through:

_____

_____

_____

_____

_____

_____

Complete the chart below:

	The person or persons X meets	What X is tempted to do or say	What X really says
1st			
2nd			
3rd			

Create an outline and write a character sketch of Yock:

Planning Guide	Character Sketch of Yock
What is Yock's state of mind when he comes to talk to his father?	
How does he explain his feelings about killing the terrorist?	
What did he want to tell his father?	
How does he respond to his father's actions?	
What do these events tell you about Yock?	

There are a plethora of MEQ styles. However, many that I have seen can be answered by using lower level thinking skills (recognition/recall), which, at least in my estimation, do not qualify as MEQs as they do not focus on concepts which require higher level thinking skills.

Appendix B

Holograms

In the scientific world, to record a hologram of a complex object, a laser beam is first split into two separate beams of light using a beam splitter of half-silvered glass or a bi-refringent material. One beam illuminates the object reflecting its image onto the recording medium as it scatters the beam. The second (reference) beam illuminates the recording medium directly.

According to diffraction theory, each point in the object acts as a source of light. Each of these point sources interferes with the reference beam, giving rise to an interference pattern. The resulting pattern is the sum of a large number (strictly speaking, an infinite number) of point source and reference beam interference patterns.

When the object is no longer present, the holographic plate is illuminated by the reference beam. Each point source diffraction grating will diffract part of the reference beam to reconstruct the wave front from the point source. These individual wave fronts add together to reconstruct the whole of the object beam.

The viewer perceives a wave front that is identical to the scattered wave front of the object illuminated by the reference beam so that it appears to him or her that the object is still in place. This image is known as a "virtual" image as it is generated even though the object is no longer there. The direction of the light source seen when illuminating the virtual image is that of the original illuminating beam.

Since each point in a hologram contains light from the whole of the original scene, the whole scene can, in principle, be reconstructed from an arbitrarily small part of the hologram. To demonstrate this concept, the hologram can be broken into small pieces and the entire object can still be seen from each small piece. If one envisions the hologram as a "window" on the subject, then each small piece of hologram is just a part of the window that can be viewed, even if the rest of the window is blocked off.

This explains, albeit in somewhat simple terms, how transmission holograms work. Other types of holograms such as rainbow and <u>Denisyuk</u> models are more complex but work by use of the same principles.

In terms of memory engrams, the auditory and visual sensory data would arrive in bits traveling in wave form that might correspond to the "points" and "wave" interference patterns making up transmission holograms. Memories associated with these senses might be recalled as the virtual "window" scenes described above. Other types of incoming senses to the brain data might use one or more of the more complex models that are thought to exist. This hypothesis might be worthy of exploring and probably is.

Note: This model of possible long-term memory structure indicates that the memory is stored at one (box-like) structure in the brain. However, recent research indicates that when one is working with long-term memories the lights go on in various parts of the brain while one is thinking. This does not seem to support the hologram concept and perhaps makes the process even more complicated.

Appendix C

Active Verbs

accelerate	describe	invest	propose
accentuate	design	investigate	prove
access	detail	invite	provide
accomplish	determine	involve	publicize
achieve	develop	know	publish
acquire	devise	label	purchase
add	devote	lack	pursue
adjust	diagnose	lead	qualify
advertise	differ	learn	quantify
advise	differentiate	lengthen	raise
alleviate	direct	lessen	rank
allow	discontinue	limit	rate
amend	discuss	link	read
amplify	dispatch	list	realize
analyze	distinguish	magnify	rebut
announce	distribute	maintain	receive
appeal	divide	make	recognize
apply	donate	manage	record
arrange	draft	manufacture	recover
articulate	duplicate	master	reduce

ask	earmark	maximize	refine
assemble	earn	measure	reflect
assess	educate	medicate	register
assimilate	elevate	merchandise	relate
assist	engage	merge	rely
authorize	ensure	mesh	remain
balance	entail	minimize	remind
beat	envision	mix	remove
become	equal	model	repair
begin	establish	modernize	replace
believe	evaluate	modify	report
belong	examine	monitor	reproduce
bring	exceed	motivate	request
build	excel	move	require
call	exemplify	need	research
cancel	exempt	negotiate	reserve
canvas	exhibit	net	resolve
carry out	expand	nominate	respond
categorize	experiment	note	restore
change	explain	nullify	restrict
check	extend	obey	result
choose	extract	obligate	retain
circumvent	find	observe	return
clarify	finish	occur	reveal
classify	focus	offer	review
close	form	omit	reward
coach	format	open	sample
collaborate	formulate	operate	search
collect	fulfill	oppose	select
combine	fund	order	sell
commend	generate	organize	send
communicate	get	orient	separate
compare	give	package	set up

compose	go	pass	show
conclude	grade	patent	signal
condense	guide	pay	sort
conduct	heighten	perfect	specify
confirm	help	perform	start
connect	hinder	perpetuate	state
constitute	identify	persuade	submit
construct	illuminate	phase in	suggest
consult	illustrate	phase out	support
contain	implement	pick	survey
continue	include	place	synthesize
contrast	incorporate	plan	systematize
contribute	increase	poll	take
cooperate	incur	portray	teach
coordinate	index	practice	test
count	indicate	prepare	tract
create	individualize	prescribe	train
cultivate	inform	preserve	transfer
cut	inspire	prevent	translate
decide	install	print	transport
dedicate	institute	process	understand
define	instruct	procure	validate
delay	intend	produce	verify
delegate	interpret	program	wish
demonstrate	interview	prohibit	work
depend	introduce	project	write
depict	invent	promote	wrote

Appendix D

Pseudo-reasoning is kind of a middle ground between unsupported claims and explicit statements. Pseudo-reasoning comprises a large and varied catalog of emotional appeals, factual irrelevancies, and persuasive devices the sometimes move people to accept or reject claims when they have no good ground for doing so. The dictionary word for pseudo-reasoning is "fallacies" and in this session that is the term which will be used.

A list of fallacies and their descriptions follow:

Smokescreen or red herring fallacy

The act of bringing in another topic that is irrelevant to a topic being discussed, which intentionally is brought up to detract from the subject being discussed.

I think the gun-control plan the administration has produced is a pretty good idea. You know, the gun-control issue is getting linked to the crime-fighting issue these days. So, if we Republicans are going to keep our reputation as the number one crime-fighting party, we are going to have to get behind this gun-control plan.

The subjectivist fallacy

When a statement made by one person is countered by the person saying 'well it may be true for you but not for me', which is to say that a statement can be true and not true at the same time. (This is a good ploy for a conversation stopper).

Hiram - You know, I've come to the conclusion that a person really needs at least 7 hours of sleep every night in order to feel healthy.

Wald - That may be true for you but it is not true for me.

Appeal to belief fallacy

The mere fact that most people believe a claim does not guarantee its truth. When weaccept other people's opinion without a good reason we are taken in by this fallacy.

Free will? Of course people have free will. Everyone believes that. It hardly seems possible not to believe it. i.e. A job in management is surely better than a job, say, as a bus driver. Just ask anybody. They'll tell you that it is better to get an education and go into management.

Common practice fallacy

The justification or defense of an action on the grounds that it is a common practice; everyone does it, or most people do it, or most people of a certain category do it.

Most people will argue that they should not have been given a speeding ticket because almost everyone drives over the limit.

Peer pressure and the bandwagon fallacy

If you support a political candidate because you think he/she is going to win instead of whatever merits they may have, you are "jumping on the bandwagon".

When you change your choice in an issue because of your want of their approval; you are submitting to peer pressure - frequently not in your best interest.

Wishful thinking fallacy

Sometimes the idea of a claim being false is so unpleasant that we decide the claim must be true simply because the alternative is so awful.

It would be so great to win the lottery. I've imagined all week how I would spend the money! I just really think I've got a chance this week.

Scare tactics fallacy

Something is said in connection with a claim that elicits or is intended to elicit a psychological response of some sort - a desire - a fear - some feeling or other emotion that may well induce acceptance of the claim.

Dear professor Finsterwald:

I would like to see you tomorrow about my final grade. I think that it was unfair and I should have gotten a better grade. My telephone number is below, so please call me. By the way, I believe you know my aunt. She's the Dean.

Appeal to pity fallacy

Actions performed out of concern for others are often rationally and ethically justified. What you have to ask your self is: if I decide based on pity, will this turn out to be something that I will regret?

Roofer- I'm positive that my work will meet your requirements. I really need the money, what with my wife being sick and all.

Appeal to anger or indignation fallacy

Sleazy politicians often use this fallacy in their campaign. This is an appeal to indignation. For example, politicians will run a picture of a well-know rapist in an ad implying the opponent supports or is like the rapist. (Unfortunately, many people buy into this fallacy).

The Bush - McCain action in the South Carolina face-off prior to the primaries; the boat issue in the Bush - Kerry campaign, etc.

Two wrongs make a right fallacy

This is a form of pseudo-reasoning that is intended to justify the claim that it is all right for A to do something harmful to B. It occurs when somebody indulges in illegitimate retaliation for a wrong imposed on him/her.

Suppose Hiram burned down Finsterwald's house because Finsterwald had put a big dent in Hiram's car when he cut down a tree and it fell on Hiram's car.

After leaving the local supermarket, Serena noticed that the sales clerk had given her too much change. "Oh well," she rationalizes, "if I had given him too much money, he wouldn't return it to me".

Appendix E

Enrichment Activities to Support 15-Minute Lectures

The dyad/triad system:

- In this strategy the teacher lectures for 15-20 minutes then poses a conceptual question/problem, based on the mini-lecture they just heard or the objective of the lecture, for students to individually think about (briefly), then to turn to another student and each take turn sharing their response. If time permits, one or more pairs (dyads) may share their responses to the class as a whole or you might follow the break with a discussion period in which you respond to the questions. Or, you might ask groups to take leadership in asking other groups to respond to the question. Or, you might ask one group to teach another group the answer to the question and why it is appropriate, or you might give a mini-lecture. Other suggestions are:

You might ask students to explain why the answer that they chose is the best answer.

You might ask students to share their responses in groups of four rather than the class.

Ask students to relate the question to a previous lesson.

Provide a question that requires prioritizing steps in the solution. Have them prioritize and explain why they did so.

Provide a question and the answer and ask students to explain why the answer is correct or why it is not. (Careful with this one – always finalize with the correct answer).

Ask students to paraphrase something in their own words.

Ask students to generate two real world examples of one or more concepts covered in the mini-lecture.

Ask students to generate one question that the students believe has yet to be addressed in the class.

- Give a **one-minute quiz** that asks the groups to summarize the two or three most important parts of the lecture so far. Have your students defend their choices and as they do use the "Why" question frequently. Grading this process – kills it!

- Run a **brainstorming** exercise either in small groups or with the entire class. Follow the rules of brainstorming: no criticizing, building on other's ideas, and record all responses on newsprint or whiteboard or an overhead projector. Brainstorming works best with questions that do not have a clear answer, i.e. concept questions. This will likely produce some substantive issues for a follow-up lecture, discussion or dyad activity.

- Another strategy is the **minute paper**. This involves asking students to briefly write out a response to two questions. The questions are: "What is the most important thing that you learned in the previous mini lecture? And, what issue in the mini lecture is not well understood?" This process could be used at the beginning of a class dealing with a reading assignment rather than the lecture.

- **Scripted group learning** is another strategy. In this process students take turns as re-caller/summarizer and checker. The re-caller summarizes the content of the prior lecture and the checker assesses the summarizer's accuracy and detail. After determining the accuracy of the summary, students jointly work on constructing strategies that would help them remember the content, i.e. constructing examples and developing mnemonic devices.

- The use of concept maps aid in understanding and remembering content. Concept maps are two-dimensional networks that interrelate important concepts. They draw student's attention to the overall structure of the lecture by creating visual clues of key topics and ideas presented in the lecture. (Biggs & Tang, p. 112) Gillis states: "Mapping operates to build and link mental spaces. Mental spaces are partial structures that proliferate when we think and talk, allowing a fine-grained partitioning of our discourse and knowledge structures. (Herbert, p.7) Dyads or other sized groups may work at one map.

There are several other possibilities for use during break or enrichment activities. Most of them follow the patterns addressed above. I am certain that all possibilities have not been discussed, even on the internet. Be creative and develop your own.

Tips for Discussion Sessions

For your 15-minute lectures, discussions, or breaks, the following question models may be of use to you to help engage the students more fully during your lectures or during the breaks:

- **Conceptual clarification questions:**

  Why are you saying that?
  What exactly does this mean?
  How does this relate to what we are talking about?
  What is the nature of ....?
  What do we already know about this?
  Can you give me an example?
  Are you saying... or ...?
  Can you rephrase that please?

- **Probing assumptions:**

  What else could we assume?
  You seem to be assuming...?

How did you choose those assumptions?

Please explain why/how...?

How can you verify or disprove that assumption?

What would happen if...?

Do you agree or disagree with...?

- **Probing rationale, reasons and evidence:**

Why is this happening?

How do you know this?

Show me...?

Can you give me an example of this?

What is the nature of this?

Are these reasons good enough?

Would it stand up in court?

How might it be refuted?

How can I be sure of what you are saying?

Why is...happening?

Why? (Keep asking it - you'll never get past a few times)

What evidence is there to support what you are saying?

On what authority are you basing your argument?

- **Questioning viewpoints and perspectives.**

Most arguments are given from a particular position. Show that there are other equally valid viewpoints.

Another way of looking at this is...does this seem reasonable?

What alternative ways of looking at this are there?

Why is...necessary?

Who benefits from this?

What is the difference between...and...?

Why is it better than...?

What are the strengths and weaknesses of...?

How are... and...similar?

What would...say about it?

What if you compared...and...?

How could you look another way at this?

- **Probe implications and consequences:**

  The argument that they give may have logical implications that can be forecast. Do these make sense? Are they desirable?

  Then what would happen?

  What are the consequences of that assumption?

  How could...be used to...?

  What are the implications of...?

  How does...effect...?

  How does...fit with what we learned before?

  Why is this important?

  What is the best? Why?

- **Question about the question:**

  What is the point of asking the question?

  Why do you think I asked this question?

  What does this mean?

Teaching Strategies to Supplement Small-Group[1] Classes:

Cooperative learning technique:

In this technique, students are given information via lectures, readings, PowerPoint presentations and so on. Teams of students are assigned to complete a worksheet, solve a problem, develop a concept map, etc. After the team work, students are tested individually to insure that teammates had tutored one another as the task was being worked on. This is one of the most teacher-centered small group processes as the instructor usually determines the composition of the groups and most other aspects of the instructional sequence.

Cooperative squared technique

This technique is structured around a series of 1–1 team building techniques. The instructor assigns a common topic to all teams within the class and identifies a series of subtopics related to the main topic.

Each student within the team selects one of the subtopics, researches it, and shares his/her findings with other members of the team. After group discussion, the information is compiled into a group presentation which is given to the entire class.

Checker-cooperative technique

This technique is similar to the cooperative squared technique, except that each student in the class is assigned a subtopic by the instructor. The student researches the subtopic and comes back to the class to discuss the subtopic with other students in the class who were assigned the same topic. Team members then go back to their original team and share their revised response with the team.

Group investigation technique

Each team is assigned or selects a different issue within a broad topic. Students are given a great deal of freedom in deciding how to organize their teams, conduct research, and present their findings to the total class. The emphasis is on higher level learning, applying and synthesizing ideas, and drawing inferences.